Money, Uncertainty and Time

T0299931

This book starts from a simple observation, namely that Keynesian economics, broadly defined as the theoretical approach that seeks inspiration in Keynes's writings, has made important contributions to the economics discipline, and remains a driving force in the development of new theories, policies and methods of analysis.

The author argues that Keynesian economists are dissenters who question the traditional proposition that market economies automatically self-adjust to the full employment level of output. He examines the role that money, uncertainty and time have played in the development of the Keynesian dissent over the last few decades. The book is divided into three main sections. Part I deals with the historical development of Keynesian economics and the lessons that can be learned from its successes and failures. Part II is concerned with the theoretical elements of modern Keynesian economics. It deals with notions of rationality, probability relations and knowledge and their applications to the theory of unemployment and the monetary circuit theory. Finally, Part III deals with the Horizontalist and the Structuralist analyses of endogenous money and the possibility of encompassing these analyses into a more general theory.

A concise and comprehensive analysis of the issues surrounding uncertainty, money and time, this informative book will be useful for all those scholars and students involved with monetary theory and policy and the history of economic thought.

Giuseppe Fontana is Professor of Monetary Economics at the University of Leeds, UK and Associate Professor of Economics at the University of Sannio, Italy.

Routledge International Studies in Money and Banking

Money, Uncertainty and Time

Giuseppe Fontana

Routledge
Taylor & Francis Group

LONDON AND NEW YORK

Transferred to digital printing 2010

First published 2009 by Routledge
2 Park Square, Milton Park, Abingdon, Oxon OX14 4RN

Simultaneously published in the USA and Canada
by Routledge
270 Madison Ave, New York, NY 10016

Routledge is an imprint of the Taylor & Francis Group, an informa business

© 2009 Giuseppe Fontana

Typeset in Times by
Keystroke, 28 High Street, Tettenhall, Wolverhampton

All rights reserved. No part of this book may be reprinted or reproduced or
utilised in any form or by any electronic, mechanical, or other means, now
known or hereafter invented, including photocopying and recording, or in
any information storage or retrieval system, without permission in writing
from the publishers.

British Library Cataloguing in Publication Data
A catalogue record for this book is available from the British Library

Library of Congress Cataloging in Publication Data
Fontana, Giuseppe
Money, uncertainty and time / Giuseppe Fontana.
p. cm.
Includes bibliographical references and index.
1. Keynesian economics. 2. Money. 3. Monetary policy. I. Title.
HB99.7.F66 2008
332.401–dc22
2008012954

ISBN10: 0–415–27960–7 (hbk)
ISBN10: 0–415–58873–1 (ebk)
ISBN10: 0–203–50329–5 (ebk)

ISBN13: 978–0–415–27960–4 (hbk)
ISBN13: 978–0–415–58873–7 (ebk)
ISBN13: 978–0–203–50329–4 (ebk)

**To Augusto and Malcolm,
from a pupil to his mentors**

Contents

PART III
Understanding endogenous money   **71**

Illustrations

Figures

Tables

Acknowledgements

Most of the arguments discussed in this book have appeared in print. However, the arguments have been explicitly rewritten for this book and, in some cases, the amount of revision and development has been substantial. I am grateful to the following publishers for their permission to use some copyright material from previously published work:

Banca Nazionale del Lavoro (BNL) Editori: 'The Future of Post Keynesian Economics', co-author Bill Gerrard, *Banca Nazionale del Lavoro Quarterly Review*, 2006, 59 (236): 49–80.

Blackwell Publishing: 'Keynes on the "Nature of Economic Thinking": The Principle of Non-Neutrality of Choice and the Principle of Non-Neutrality of Money', *American Journal of Economics and Sociology*, 2001, 60(4): 711–743. 'Endogenous Money: An Analytical Approach', co-author Ezio Venturino, *Scottish Journal of Political Economy*, 2003, 50(4): 398–416. 'Rethinking Endogenous Money: A Constructive Interpretation of the Debate between Accommodationists and Structuralists', *Metroeconomica*, 2004, 55(4): 367–385.

Edward Elgar: 'Disequilibrium States and Adjustment Processes: Towards a Historical-Time Analysis of Behaviour Under Uncertainty', co-author Bill Gerrard, in Sheila Dow and Peter Earl (eds), *Contingency, Complexity and the Theory of Firm: Essays in Honour of Brian Loasby*, 1999, vol. 2, pp. 235–253, Edward Elgar, Cheltenham.

Oxford University Press: 'Hicks on Monetary Theory and History: Money as *Endogenous* Money', *Cambridge Journal of Economics*, 2004, 28 (1): 73–88.

Routledge – Taylor & Francis: 'Disequilibrium States and Adjustment Processes: Towards a Historical-Time Analysis of Behaviour Under Uncertainty', co-author Bill Gerrard, *Philosophical Psychology*, 1999, 12(3):

311–324. 'The Encompassing Principle as an Emerging Methodology for Post Keynesian Economics', co-author Bill Gerrard, in Philip Arestis, Meghnad Desai and Sheila Dow (eds), *Methodology, Microeconomics and Keynes: Essays in Honour of Victoria Chick*, 2002, vol. 2, pp. 95–105, Routledge, London. 'Post Keynesian Approaches to Endogenous Money: A Time Framework Explanation', *Review of Political Economy*, 2003, 15(3): 291–314.

M.E.Sharpe: 'Post Keynesians and Circuitists on Money and Uncertainty: An Attempt at Generality', *Journal of Post Keynesian Economics*, 2000, 23(1): 27–48.

Every effort has been made to trace all the copyright holders, but if any have been inadvertently overlooked, Routledge will be pleased to make the necessary arrangments at the first opportunity.

The book was mostly written during my research sabbatical leave period in the Spring of 2005 at the Centre for Full Employment and Price Stability (C-FEPS), University of Missouri Kansas City (UMKC), Kansas City, USA, and it was completed during my research period as 2008 Shackle scholar and visiting fellow at St Edmund's College and the Cambridge Centre for Economic and Public Policy (CCEPP), University of Cambridge, Cambridge. I would like to express appreciation to members of these institutions, especially Randall (Randy) Wray, Mat Forstater, Paul Luzio, John McCombie and Philip Arestis for providing a stimulating and pleasant working environment.

I am also sincerely indebted to Philip Arestis, Victoria (Vicky) Chick, Sheila Dow, Geoff Harcourt, Ian Edwards and Malcolm Sawyer for reading the entire manuscript, and for their extremely helpful comments and constructive criticisms. I have acted on some, but by no means all, of their suggestions.

I would also like to thank Paul Dalziel, Paul Davidson, Bill Gerrard, Augusto Graziani, Eckhard Hein, Peter Howells, John King, Jan Kregel, Marc Lavoie, Basil Moore, Alain Parguez, Steve Pressman, Riccardo Realfonzo, Louis-Philippe Rochon, Sergio Rossi, Roy Rotheim, Mario Seccareccia, John Smithin, Pavlina Tcherneva, Eric Tymoigne and Randall (Randy) Wray for comments and suggestions concerning different parts of the book. Many thanks also go to Rob Langham, Terry Clague and their colleagues at Routledge for endless support through this project. It goes without saying that friends and colleagues mentioned above are not responsible for any remaining errors in the book. For these, I am alone responsible.

My family has consistently supported me in all endeavours. Without their generosity and love, this book would not have been written. From my first arrival in England to the present, Peter Clarke has been amicable landlord, spiritual mentor and devoted friend. For all this I am very grateful. In the final stages of completing the manuscript I met Aurelie Charles, who has changed my life a lot and helped my work on this book considerably by doing the lion's share of making the arrangements for our wedding celebrations in Italy and France!

Giuseppe Fontana
St Edmund's College
Cambridge, Spring 2008

Preface

This book is the long overdue publication of my PhD thesis completed at the University of Leeds under the supervision of Malcolm Sawyer, and examined in the Spring of 1999 by Geoff Harcourt (University of Cambridge), and Sheila Dow (University of Stirling). The book draws also on my Italian PhD thesis completed at the University Federico II of Naples, under the supervision of Augusto Graziani in the Winter of 1996.

I offer my most sincere apologies to the readers for the long publication delay, due a variety of reasons, including the pressure for young scholars to produce journal articles rather than books, and some personal reluctance to go back to my original doctoral typescript. I hope that the long gestation period has helped to make the arguments clearer and sharper.

Foreword

I am delighted to be able to write a Foreword to Giuseppe Fontana's fine book. I first met Giuseppe near the time I was to be one of the examiners of his PhD dissertation at Leeds from which his book has developed. I was most taken then by his enthusiasm, scholarship, powerful analytical mind and economic intuition, not to mention his basic humanity, kindness and courtesy. We have since kept in touch and my first impressions have been confirmed – more than – time and again. Giuseppe is the best sort of scholar and political economist. He has deep understanding of the important contributions in our subject, he is generous, and when critical always sympathetic and positive as well. He is a conciliator without sacrificing either logic or his own point of view. His book builds on his understanding of the various strands of Post Keynesianism as well as on the seminal contributions of Keynes and Kalecki themselves. As with Keynes, so, too, Giuseppe is first and foremost a monetary economist in that he is fascinated by the integration of credit and money, and the institutions they necessitate, with the dominant economic processes of distribution, employment, growth and pricing over time. Again, as with Marx, he is deeply aware of the need for macro-economic foundations of microeconomics arising from aggregate demand and aggregate supply, production interdependence and the aggregate aspects of credit creation and the supply of money. He has made an especially important contribution by bringing out clearly the approaches, within the endogenous money literature, of those he has dubbed the Horizontalists and the Structuralists, telling us how they differ in emphasis, yet may be combined together in a more full analysis of the workings of a monetary production economy. In doing so he shows himself to be a true intellectual son of Maynard Keynes, the more so because the end point of his endeavours is the creation of practical and effective policy measures. Giuseppe has also done us a service by reiterating the place that methodology plays in the contrast between mainstream and post-Keynesian approaches. While I would prefer to have seen more emphasis on Marx's contributions in his exposition of this, I do not believe Giuseppe and I need to be at loggerheads. As he knows I think the core truths of critical realism, to which he is attracted, derived from Marx's methodology and indeed, from all good scientific practice in the social sciences. Be that as it may, I am extremely happy to recommend this scholarly, enthusiastic and original volume to its readers. So please read on.

G.C. Harcourt
Jesus College
Cambridge
May 2007

1 Introduction

Money, uncertainty and time

This book starts from a simple observation, namely that Keynesian economics, broadly defined as the theoretical approach that seeks inspiration in Keynes's writings, has made important contributions to the economics discipline, and it remains a driving force in the development of new theories and methods of analysis. For instance, in his Nobel Prize lecture in December 2001, George Akerlof explained that the research programme for which he received the prestigious prize was nothing but the development of behavioural macroeconomics in the original spirit of Keynes's *General Theory* (1936) (Akerlof 2002: 411). He also referred to the diminished authority of Keynesian economics from the late-1960s and 1970s together with the resurgence of Classical economics as a significant development in the history of the economics discipline. For all the progress on the microeconomic foundations of price and wage decisions, New Classical macroeconomics failed to account for real-world phenomena such as involuntary unemployment and rising income inequalities (see also Stiglitz 2002: 489). Akerlof concludes his review of modern theories that explicitly attempt to provide explanations for, and solutions to, these real-world phenomena by stating that Keynes's work was a major driving force in the development of New Keynesian theories, and more generally the greatest contribution to behavioural economics before the present era. This profound vitality of Keynesian economics is indicative of the significance of Keynes's insights into the working of modern economies. It confirms the high reference power of economic ideas that have had to face, and consequently be adapted to, a variety of often very different historical circumstances.

The term Keynesian economics has usually been used to label the core theoretical ideas of Keynes's *magnum opus*, *The General Theory of Employment, Interest and Money* (1936), and its policy implications (Eatwell 1987: 46–47, Kregel 1987a). More precisely, Keynesian economics has usually been associated with the tendency to replace changes in the interest rate and other prices, with changes in the level of national income as the main factor of adjustment between investment and saving. In Keynesian analysis, income effects take priority over price changes in the process of formation of the overall level of output and employment. This idea was directly derived from the principle of effective demand, which downplayed the price mechanism, and promoted, via the multiplier analysis, the link between autonomous expenditure (e.g. investment) and income. This view leads to the conclusion that in a market economy there is no automatic tendency either in the short or long period[1] ensuring that the level of output corresponds to the full employment level. The economy could thus reach an equilibrium position with output far below capacity.

In terms of policy formation, this means that it should be the responsibility of the government to intervene in the economy by managing, via fiscal and monetary policies, a level of aggregate demand that would generate full employment. The distinctive features of Keynesian economics can thus be summarised into three basic propositions (Fontana and Gerrard 2006).

Proposition I (the possibility of involuntary unemployment): the economy does not automatically and effectively self-adjust towards the social macroeconomic optimum.

Proposition II (the principle of effective demand): aggregate demand plays an important role in determining the adjustment path of the economy.

Proposition III (the principle of policy effectiveness): fiscal and monetary policies are effective for determining, under certain circumstances, the level of output and employment in the economy.

Propositions I–III serve two purposes. First, they are useful for defining Keynesian economics vis-à-vis Neoclassical economics. From this perspective, Keynesian economists are dissenters who question the characteristic Neoclassical proposition that market economies automatically self-adjust to

---

1 This book does not distinguish between short run and short period (or similarly long run and long period), though consistency with English language and the Marshallian tradition of studying economics in Cambridge would require me to use 'run' for an historical interval of time, and 'period' for an analytical interval of time (Marshall 1890: 363–380): '"period" is an analytical concept where the economist is in control of what may vary and what is locked up, at least provisionally, in the *ceteris paribus* pound; "run", by contrast, is an historical concept where whatever is either changing or constant in a given situation is an historical outcome' (Harcourt 2006: 62, n. 6). In accordance with modern practice, in this book short-run and long-run refer to the analytical intervals of time (however see, on the risks of this modern practice, Panico and Petri 1987).

the full employment level of output. In Neoclassical economics involuntary employment is a logically untenable position (Dixon 2000). Could not unemployed workers obtain a job if only they were willing to reduce their reservation wage? The answer of Keynesian economists to this question is no. Involuntarily unemployed workers are willing to accept, but cannot obtain, jobs identical to those currently held by workers with identical ability. Involuntary unemployment is a meaningful concept, and it gives strength to the principles of effective demand and policy effectiveness.

Second, Propositions I–III are an effective way to introduce the particular contributions made by different interpreters of Keynesian economics. For instance, the distinct position of the scholars discussed in this book, the Post Keynesian economists, is to accept the possibility of involuntary unemployment (Proposition I), and to argue that aggregate demand affects the adjustment path of the economy, which also impacts on any equilibrium position which may or may not be reached (Proposition II). Furthermore, Post Keynesian economists maintain that aggregate demand has long-run effects on economic activities; hence by managing fiscal and monetary policies, the government can generate a satisfactory level of output and employment (Proposition III). By contrast, New Keynesian economists qualify their interpretations of the Keynesian propositions in terms of the distinction between short-run and long-run models. In the former, New Keynesian economists support Propositions I–III, but in the latter they revert to the Neoclassical principle that market economies automatically self-adjust to the full employment level of output. For this reason, New Keynesian economists are usually sceptical about the long-run real effects of changes in the components of aggregate demand, and the role of stabilisation policies, more generally. In brief, Propositions I–III serve the dual objectives of broadly defining Keynesian economics vis-à-vis Neoclassical economics, and of allowing for different interpretations of Keynesian economics. This second objective has an immediate application for the purpose of this intro-ductory chapter, since it helps to explain the fact that the nature of Keynesian dissent has always been a source of debate.

Keynes himself presented the publication of the *General Theory* as a challenge to the economic establishment, a frontal attack on Classical theory (Keynes 1935a). However, in the same book Keynes asserts that 'if our central controls succeed in establishing an aggregate volume of output corresponding to full employment as nearly as is practicable, the Classical theory comes into its own again from this point onwards' (Keynes 1936: 378). This seductive, if arguably contradictory, position towards Classical and then Neoclassical economics has also been an important feature of the historical development of Keynesian economics. Over the past decades, several economists have claimed to be inspired by Keynes's ideas, but many more have clearly also been so inspired. Several approaches have been put forward claiming to have made important contributions to the development of Keynesian economics. Yet, during this time wide divergences have emerged over the degree to which Neoclassical economics must be rejected or extended in order to accommodate the Keynesian Propositions I–III.

On one side, it has been argued that the different interpretations of Keynesian economics reflect the evolution of the economic discipline. As the discipline has evolved, the nature of the Keynesian dissent vis-à-vis Neoclassical economics has changed. On the other side, it has been suggested that the sheer scale and complexity of Keynes's writings explain the emergence of several Keynesian approaches. Different Keynesian scholars have been inspired by different writings and, as in the case of the *General Theory*, even by different chapters of the same work. Whatever the cause, the vigour and changing forms of Keynesian economics are indicative of the high reference power of the three Keynesian propositions. This also means that it is beyond the scope of this book to present and evaluate in any depth the numerous and influential contributions that have usually been associated with Keynesian economics. The objective of this book is indeed more modest. The book looks at a specific research programme within Keynesian economics, namely the Post Keynesian approach. Even with this limitation, the scope of the book would still be vast, so the book mainly aims to provide a coherent framework for assessing recent contributions to the monetary stream of Post Keynesian economics. In the next section some possible reasons for the emergence of several approaches to Keynesian economics are briefly discussed, before concluding with an overview of the book's content.

The changing nature of the Keynesian dissent

The nature and origin of the Keynesian dissent vis-à-vis Neoclassical economics has always been a source of much debate. A common explanation for this debate is the lack of common purpose in Keynesian dissent, which simply illustrates the way in which a discipline like economics evolves over time (e.g. Laidler 1999). According to this evolutionary view, before attaining recognition into mainstream economics, it is obvious that the relationship between any new theory and existing theories needs to be explored. Then, the novelty and importance of the new theory must be conveyed to other practitioners, and finally to policy-makers and the public at large. Therefore, in the process of being absorbed into mainstream economics the new theory loses some of its original features, and new attributes are added. From this perspective, it is not surprising that Keynesian ideas as represented by Propositions I–III have taken on forms that Keynes may have not foreseen, or that he may not have encouraged (see, for a similar conclusion, Coddington 1976). Along these lines, it is also argued that this process of absorption of Keynesian ideas into economics is a dynamic ever-changing process. In other words, if economics is continually evolving, it is natural that the nature and the forms of dissent within the discipline would also change over time.

However, this book subscribes to the view that there is much more to Keynesian dissent than is allowed by an evolutionary explanation. The 'Cambridge–Cambridge Capital Theory Controversies' over the concepts of aggregate capital and the economic meaning of capital are a case in point. Cohen and Harcourt (2003) have argued that the Capital Theory Controversies highlighted more than the logical problems of using the concept of aggregate capital in price theory. What was really at stake was the problematic issue of different ideologies and visions in economics. How best could the accumulation process in a capitalist society be envisaged and modelled? On one side, there was the Keynesian tradition pointing towards the role of competing social groups in the economic process. This was the world of entrepreneurs and capitalists defining the so-called monetary context of behaviour (Fontana and Gerrard 2002b), in which accumulation, production and exchange activities are undertaken to achieve monetary, not commodity, returns (Keynes's M-C-M' economy; see Keynes (1979: 81), and related discussion in Chapter 5 below). On the other side, there was the Neoclassical tradition of the utility-maximising agent. In the orthodox spirit of this tradition, the capital theory controversies prompted refinements and further amendments to the original price theory.

For the closest colleagues and followers of Keynes the outcome of these controversies called into question the general use of the Neoclassical approach to economics. In particular, Joan Robinson lamented that the original purpose of Keynes's work had been completely misunderstood. Keynes had presented the *General Theory* as the final result of a long struggle to escape from the old Neoclassical modes of thought and expression (Keynes 1936: xxiii). As Keynes explained in the one-page-long Chapter 1 of the *General Theory*, the fatal flaw of the Neoclassical approach lay in the nature of the axioms that were necessary to demonstrate the self-correcting tendency of the economic system. These axioms have been asserted, more often implicitly than explicitly, as universal truths. By contrast, the restricted applicability of these axioms meant that important economic phenomena such as prolonged mass unemployment could not be explained by Neoclassical theory. For this reason, Keynes felt the need to develop a less restrictive, axiomatic theory of unemployment, namely the *General Theory*.

I have called this book the *General Theory of Employment, Interest and Money*, placing the emphasis on the prefix *general*. The object of such a title is to contrast the character of my arguments and conclusions with those of the *classical* theory of the subject. . . . I shall argue that the postulates of the classical theory are applicable to a special case only and not to the general case. . . . Moreover, the characteristics of the special case assumed by the classical theory happen not to be those of the economic society in which we actually live. . . .

(Keynes 1936: 3, italics in the original)

Robinson argued forcefully that what the process of absorption into the mainstream had done was to transform the *General Theory* and related writings into a special case of the general Neoclassical theory of employment, interest and money. Keynesian economics had become synonymous with the economics of depressions and equilibrium unemployment. Keynesian economics was simply the application of the general Neoclassical theory to the restrictive case of less-than-full-employment equilibrium (Robinson 1971, see also Davidson 1994: 292, Pasinetti 1999: 22).

Another explanation for the lack of commonality in Keynesian dissent is the scale and complexity of Keynes's writings.[2] *The Collected Writings of John Maynard Keynes* number 30 volumes. Moreover, the interpretation of this large number of writings entails a lot of difficulties, not least because of the peculiar tradition of studying economics at Cambridge. Several scholars have often argued that, like many of his Cambridge colleagues, Keynes had a very practical view of economics (Harcourt 1998: 335, see also Kaldor 1982a: 3, Pasinetti 2005). Keynes was mostly concerned with the effective working of actual economic systems within a well-defined institutional structure. His analysis proceeded more on the basis of intuition than of a rigid theoretical system. For the sake of exploring his intuition, Keynes would thus accept established theories, without questioning their fundamental principles, until such questioning was forced on him by the search for consistency between the established model and his own intuitive reasoning. Therefore, his writings relate sometimes to first principles, sometimes to practical circumstances and sometimes to both. This multi-dimensional aspect of Keynes's writings has therefore allowed scholars to focus on different parts of his writings or, as is the case of the *General Theory*, on different chapters of the same work. As a result of this hetero-

---

2   It cannot be excluded that a further cause for the lack of commonality in Keynesian dissent is the natural ambiguity that results from the development of Keynes's own ideas over time.

geneity of sources, the Keynesian challenge to the Classical concept of the invisible hand has assumed a variety of forms and meanings, including *IS LM* Keynesianism, Disequilibrium Keynesianism, New Keynesianism and Fundamentalist Keynesianism. And it does not stop there. Today, Fundamentalist Keynesianism is called Post Keynesianism, which in a broad definition includes Neo-Ricardian Keynesianism, Kaleckian Keynesianism, Monetary Circuit Keynesianism and, for want of a better name, Non-ergodic/ Monetary Keynesianism[3] (Hodgson 1989, King 2003). An example may help to illustrate how the multi-dimensional aspect of Keynes's writings has affected the different nature of these 'Keynesianisms'.

Coddington has used the term 'Fundamentalist Keynesianism' to describe the work of Post Keynesian scholars like Joan Robinson and George Shackle, who believed that the analysis of the effects of uncertainty on investment in Chapter 12 of the *General Theory* was the essence of Keynes's theory (Coddington 1976: 1259–1263). In this case, Coddington is making a dual claim. First, for Post Keynesian economists, the writings of Keynes are related mostly, if not exclusively, to first principles. Second, uncertainty is a first principle informing Keynes's dissent against the invisible hand theorem, and hence it represents the guiding principle for the development of the Post Keynesian dissenting view. Other commentators have preferred to underplay the role of first principles, and focused on the practical circumstances that have guided some of the most popular writings of Keynes. In particular, it is well known that by the early 1930s Keynes felt that worldwide mass unemployment was a serious and persistent problem in urgent need of a new economic solution. For this purpose, he embarked on the writing of the *General Theory*. The possibility of mass unemployment, now as then, has thus become one of the main features of the Keynesian dissent. As uncontroversial as this proposition could be, it has become a source of great dispute between New Keynesian and Post Keynesian economists. For example, Dixon (2000) describes the New Keynesian dissent in terms of theoretical explanations for the existence in our modern economies of nominal rigidities and less-than-perfect information that give rise to the phenomenon of involuntary unemployment (among other phenomena). According to Dixon, the appeal to the Keynesian result of involuntary

---

3 By Non-ergodic/Monetary Keynesianism what is meant is the work of those Post Keynesians like Victoria Chick, Paul Davidson and Jan Kregel who have considered Keynes's insights on money and uncertainty as major contributions to economic theory (see, for example, Davidson 1972, Chick 1983, and Kregel 1987b). It is this monetary stream of Post Keynesian economics that is the major focus of this book. On the 'ergodic hypothesis' and 'non-ergodic hypothesis', see Samuelson (1968: 11–12) and Davidson (1982–83), respectively.

unemployment has set the agenda for the New Keynesian dissent. In this sense, whatever the nature of the first principles adopted, New Keynesian scholars believe that the real world keeps on revealing itself more on the side of Keynes than on the side of Neoclassical economics. It may indeed be argued that New Keynesian economics shares the same first principles as Neoclassical economics, but it differs from the latter since it considers nominal rigidities and less-than-perfect information as stylised macro-economic facts in urgent need of (microeconomic) explanations (Rotheim 1998). For this reason, most Post Keynesians have called into question the Keynesian dissent in New Keynesian economics. According to Davidson and Post Keynesian economists more generally, the Keynesian dissent is related to first principles, and therefore the New Keynesian attempt to forge Keynesian results from the axiomatic principles of Neoclassical economics is wrong-headed. As Davidson has aptly put it, where is the Keynesian beef in New Keynesian economics (Davidson 1994: 290)? In short, differences over the degree to which Neoclassical economics must be rejected or extended in order to accommodate Keynesian ideas can be explained to a certain degree by the multi-dimensional aspects of Keynes's writings. Since those writings are related in part to first principles, and in part to practical circumstances, different Keynesian economists have given different weight to these two features in their theories.

This multi-dimensional aspect of Keynes's writings has been a controversial issue not only between different Keynesian schools, but also within some of them. In particular, it has led to the emergence of a variety of theories and methods of analysis within Post Keynesian economics. Coddington has expounded the view that Fundamentalist Keynesians relate Keynes's writings mostly, if not exclusively, to first principles (Coddington 1976). This view is now well accepted by Post Keynesian scholars (e.g. Gerrard 2003). However, what those first principles are and how they should be used for the development of the Post Keynesian dissent is not yet clear. In particular, are these first principles related to economic theory, methodology or policy issues, or to all of these facets together? The aim of this book is to provide an answer to these questions by arguing that money, uncertainty and time are three important first principles of Post Keynesian dissent and that these principles are related to economic theory and methodology.

Outline of the book

The book is divided into three parts. Part I sets the frame of reference for the remaining chapters of the book. It deals with the historical development of Post Keynesian economics and the lessons that can be learned from its successes and failures. In the previous section it has been argued that Keynesian economists are dissenters who question the characteristic Classical/Neoclassical proposition that market economies automatically self-adjust to the full employment level of output. In Chapter 2 the nature of the Post Keynesian dissent is analysed in its historical evolution through what have been labelled the 'romantic age' and the 'age of uncertainty'. The former describes the period of optimism and excitement of the 1960s and 1970s, when Post Keynesian economics was considered to be an original theoretical system on the brink of replacing the dominant Neoclassical paradigm. The latter refers to the period of doubt and deep internal divisions, which followed the intense debate of the 1980s and early 1990s on the methodolical features of Post Keynesian economics. For this reason, Chapter 3 is devoted to the intimate relationship between theory and methodology in economics. In particular, Chapter 3 deals with the old debate between Keynes and the 'Classics' and its relevance for modern economics. It is often argued that Keynes and Classical economists were saying different things. But how, and why, did Keynes and the 'Classics' say these different things? Chapter 18 of the *General Theory* (Keynes 1936) is used as a case study to provide an answer to this question. From this perspective, Chapter 18 represents much more than the summary of Keynes's theory of employment and output. It restates an innovative theory of employment and income, together with the original methodology that grounds it.

Part II is concerned with the theoretical elements of Post Keynesian economics. It builds on the particular nature of the link between theory and methodology in Keynes and Post Keynesian economics discussed in Part I. It deals with the notions of rationality, probability relations and knowledge and their applications to the modern Post Keynesian theory of unemployment and the monetary circuit theory. Drawing on Keynes's work, Chapter 4 develops a theory of individual knowledge based on a two-dimensional approach to probability theory, namely probability relations and weight of argument. Probability relations provide a rational assessment of the relative degree of belief attached to alternative propositions, whereas the weight of argument measures the evidential base of these degrees of belief. These two components of probability theory allow for a general theory of individual knowledge, which includes the cases of certainty and risk as well as the case of uncertainty. Chapter 5 uses this original general theory of individual knowledge to enrich the theory of unemployment and the monetary circuit theory in Post Keynesian economics. When the evidential base of the degrees of belief is inconclusive, a probability relation cannot be conceived. This means that there is nothing to guide individuals in their practical decision-making. This situation describes the notion of uncertainty on which the demand for a liquid store of wealth is based. In these circumstances money becomes a bottomless sink of purchasing power, with the result that the economic system may settle in equilibrium at a level that falls a long way short of generating full employment. Similarly, when there is some evidential base for the degrees of belief, a probability relation can be conceived. However, given the incompleteness of the evidential base, this means that the probability relation is an unreliable guide to decision-making. This describes a different, but no less important, notion of uncertainty. In this case uncertainty is related to the existence of institutions, contracts and a final means of payment that helps to meet and alleviate the problems of exchanging goods and services, when agents face the genuine possibility of defaulting on their obligations. In other words, money, contracts and institutions define the context of modern production and speculative processes.

Finally, Part III applies the set of ideas and notions discussed in Part II to the modern debate on the endogenous money theory. It is concerned with the vagueness of human knowledge, the organic nature of economic phenomena and their significance for the use of dynamic methods in monetary theory. It deals with the Horizontalist and the Structuralist analyses of endogenous money and the possibility of encompassing these analyses into a more general theory. In Chapter 6 some of the writings on money and time of the early Hicks, as well as of the late and more critical Hicks, are discussed. In particular, the original distinction between a single-period theory and a continuation theory is explored. The former aims at simple and stable relationships that may be obscured, or at best difficult to disentangle, once all the complexities of the modern monetary economies are considered. A single period analysis is based on the simplifying assumption that within the period considered agents hold constant expectations. This assumption helps to interpret real causal structures as temporally stable, though not inherently predictable, and in this way it helps to detect mechanisms and tendencies regulating actual events. A continuation theory is the natural complement to a single-period theory. It is concerned with the effects of the events of a single period upon expectations and plans that themselves determine the events of successive single periods. In other words, a continuation theory is the study of linkages between single periods. This original methodological distinction is used in Chapter 8 to analyse the most prominent and often controversial features of the modern endogenous money theory, namely the debit–credit nature of modern money, the role of the banking system in the production and accumulation process and the origin of recent financial innovations. An overview of the modern endogenous money theory is provided in Chapter 7. The chapter starts with an analysis of the Horizontalist (also called accommodationist) approach, which historically represents the first wave of modern contributions to the endogenous money theory. The Horizontalist analysis is based on two tenets, namely that 'loans create deposits' and 'deposits generate reserves'. These two tenets are explored through an analysis of the balance sheets of commercial banks and the central bank. Next, it follows a discussion of the Structuralist analysis, which has clarified and refined some features of the Horizontalist analysis. From the perspective defended in this book, the Structuralist analysis is in fact a natural development of the early Horizontalist theory of the endogenous money. The Structuralist analysis retains the above-stated two original tenets of endogenous money theory, but these tenets are now interpreted in the light of a more explicit consideration of the liquidity preference of the agents involved in the money supply process, namely households, firms, commercial banks and the central bank. The complementary nature of the Horizontalist and the Structuralist analyses of endogenous money are further explored, with the help of an original four-panel diagram, in Chapter 8. As mentioned above, the methodological distinction between a single period analysis and a continuation analysis introduced in Chapter 6 is now used to lend support to the argument that the Horizontalist and the Structuralist analyses can be encompassed into a more general theory of endogenous money. From this perspective, the current disagreements between Horizontalists and Structuralists stem from the particular assumptions made about the general state of expectations of economic agents. Horizontalists rely upon a single period analysis that is built on the assumption that the state of expectations of all agents involved in the money supply process is constant. This assumption enables the specification of stable functional relationships that continuously changing expectations would make very laborious to specify. On the other hand, Structuralists depend on a continuation framework that explicitly takes account of the fact that the state of expectations of agents may change in the light of realised events. In this way, Structuralists are able to tackle controversial issues related to shifting monetary policies, the liquidity preference of banks and the loans-deposits nexus that are overlooked by Horizontalists. Whether the Horizontalist analysis or the Structuralist analysis is more useful or relevant depends on the purpose of the analysis, and which assumption about the general state of expectations of economic agents is more realistic in the situation analysed. In other words, it is perfectly proper, and in fact recommended, to use say Horizontalist analysis to study the reserve market in reasonably stable economic and financial conditions, and the Structuralist analysis when conditions are unstable and continuously changing.

Part I

Keynes, the 'Classics' and the modern Keynesian dissent

.

2 The historical development of dissent in Keynesian economics[1]

Introduction

In Chapter 1 it was argued that Keynesian economists are dissenters who question the characteristic Neoclassical proposition that market economies automatically self-adjust to the full employment level of output. It has also been argued that starting from its origin in the middle 1930s the Keynesian dissent has assumed a variety of forms and meanings, including *IS-LM* Keynesianism, Disequilibrium Keynesianism, New Keynesianism and Post Keynesianism. Drawing on recently published biographies of Keynes (e.g. Davidson 2007, Dostaler 2007) and new historical accounts of early Post Keynesian contributions (e.g. King 2003, also Harcourt 2006, Pasinetti 2007), this chapter examines the origins and the historical development of dissent in Post Keynesian economics. The distinction between the romantic age and the age of uncertainty is proposed. The former describes the period of optimism and excitement of the 1960s and 1970s, when Post Keynesian economics was seen as a comprehensive theoretical system alternative to the dominant Neoclassical paradigm. The end of this period was marked by an increasing awareness of the importance of the methodological features of the new paradigm. Post Keynesian economics was still viewed as possessing the potential to become an alternative to the dominant paradigm, but the transformation came to be considered more fundamental than initially envisaged. Post Keynesian economics had now to be an alternative theoretical and methodological paradigm to Neoclassical economics. This awareness of the methodological features of Post Keynesian economics initiated a period of doubt and deep internal divisions, the age of uncertainty, which still exists today. The chapter concludes discussing what lessons can be learned from the successes and failures of the romantic age and the age of uncertainty.

---

1 This chapter draws on an extensive research project with Bill Gerrard (University of Leeds) on the nature and modern developments of Post Keynesian economics.

The origins of Post Keynesian economics

Post Keynesian economics originated in the work of Joan Robinson and other Cambridge economists who sought to develop Keynes's legacy.[2] In the *General Theory*, Keynes had assumed that the stock of capital and the technique of production were given. However, as early as 1937, Robinson was already trying to move beyond Keynes's short-run approach to unemployment (Robinson 1937). At around the same time, Roy Harrod was attempting to construct a dynamic macroeconomic model. In the tradition of Keynes's masterpiece, he showed that divergences in a one-commodity economy between the equilibrium or 'warranted' rate of growth of output (G_w) and the actual rate of growth (G) instead of being self-correcting would be self-aggravating. This is what came to be known as Harrod's knife-edge problem (Harrod 1939: 22).

The LSE graduate (and staff member) but soon-converted Keynesian, Nicholas Kaldor, also made several somewhat brief contributions to the development of Post Keynesian economics (Thirlwall 1987). He suggested moving away from Keynes's use, at times, of the assumption of the money stock as an exogenous variable under the control of the central bank (Kaldor 1939: 14). Furthermore, he explored the role of the relative shares of wages and profits in maintaining macroeconomic stability (Kaldor 1940). Similar questions were also at the heart of the work of the Polish economist Michal Kalecki. He had already made important contributions to the theory of economic fluctuations before the publication of the *General Theory* (Kalecki 1939, orig. 1933), and according to Joan Robinson he was very influential in creating a Classical-Marxist interpretation of Keynes's work (Robinson 1942, see also Targetti and Kinda-Hass 1982).

During the Second World War, and especially throughout the post-war period, these initial efforts at the theory of growth, and the long-period implications of the principle of effective demand continued. Linked to this work, there was an increasing focus on the income distribution in an economy with two separate economic groups: workers, who receive wages, and capitalists, who receive profits. Again, for his theory of employment Keynes did not need a theory of distribution. But by now, his followers felt

---

2   Joan Robinson has also provided the most succinct and extraordinarily modern definition of Post Keynesian economics: 'To me, the expression *post-Keynesian* has a definite meaning; it applies to an economic theory or method of analysis which takes account of the difference between the future and the past' (Robinson 1978: 12, italics in the original). For a thorough and thoughtful account of the evolution of Post Keynesian economics, from its origins in the interpretations of the *General Theory* (Keynes 1936) to the present, see King (2002), and the related discussion of the book in Davidson (2003), and Post Keynesianism (2005).

that they could not separate growth from distribution issues. The suspicion was that post-war growth had not overcome absolute poverty: rather it seemed to have increased it. Growth and distribution were thus seen as being intimately related.

These theoretical analyses of growth and distribution culminated in Robinson's masterpiece *The Accumulation of Capital* (Robinson 1956). Robinson had actually first aired some of her ideas in an extended review of Harrod's lectures on dynamic economics (Harrod 1948). There, among other criticisms, she complained that the 'natural' or maximum rate of growth of output (G_n) is not a natural datum. This rate depends on the increase in the working population and on the increase in output-per-head due to technical progress. Thus, she argued, G_n can be, and indeed is, affected by policy-making and aggregate demand (Robinson 1949: 85). Some of these ideas were further developed in Robinson's masterpiece (1956). The core of the book is the idea that chances and changes in the development of an economy depend partly on technical progress and partly on social institutions and political power. At the end of the book, she also located in the different propensity to save out of profits and wages an important way of overcoming the 'knife-edge' problem (Robinson 1956: 405–406). Unfortunately, the book did not make much impact on the economics profession; neither did her *Essays in the Theory of Economic Growth* (Robinson 1962).

Arguably, Kaldor's writings on distribution and growth had better fortune. Certainly, his 'Alternative theories of distribution' (Kaldor 1956) was to become a very popular reading in Post Keynesian economics. The first part of the paper is a profound critique of the Neoclassical theory of distribution showing that the marginal productivity theory of factor pricing and distribution is based on assumptions that are both unrealistic and too restrictive. The second part of the paper is Kaldor's macroeconomic model of relative income shares. The core argument is that, as long as prices are flexible and the marginal propensity to save out of profits is greater than the propensity to save out of wages, investment determines the relationship between wages and profits. Furthermore, with the additional assumption that the share of investment in income is constant, the share of profits will also remain constant over time. In this way, Kaldor accounted for the historically relative stability of distributive shares, a key 'stylised' fact of our economies, in his own words. However, his theory was based on the assumption of full employment, a rather un-Keynesian assumption, and that remains the main limitation of Kaldor's distribution theory.

The independent investment function also played an important role in Kaldor's growth theory (Kaldor 1957). Again, starting off with an initial critique of Neoclassical growth theory, Kaldor tried to show that steady growth equilibrium is inconsistent with a less-than-full employment condition. In fact, as a result of underemployment, changes in the relationship between wages and prices would follow such that profit and real wage shares would be made consistent with steady growth. One of the main deficiencies of this model and its further modification (e.g. Kaldor and Mirrlees 1962) is the highly aggregative level of analysis with quasi-exclusive focus on the manufacturing sector. For this reason, as explained by his biographer Thirlwall (1987: 174), from 1966 onwards Kaldor adopted a sectoral approach to his writings on economic growth (see, for example, Kaldor 1966, 1970a).

The development of alternative Keynesian theories of economic growth and income distribution slowly began to take a methodological turn. These theories, often implicitly, rejected the marginalist microfoundations of rational-agent models and instead used aggregate behavioural functions to represent socio-economic realities. The rejection of marginalist theorising ultimately became the principal issue in the 'Cambridge–Cambridge Capital Theory Controversies' (Harcourt 1972). The Controversies attracted eminent economists such as Pasinetti, Robinson and Sraffa on one side, versus Samuelson, Solow and Hahn on the other. The Controversies started with Robinson's 'The production function and the theory of capital' (Robinson 1953–54), reaching their climax with Sraffa's classic *The Production of Commodities by Means of Commodities* (Sraffa 1960), and ended with Bliss's *Capital Theory and the Distribution of Income* (1975). In the intervening years several papers were published by the above eminent economists and many more by others in first-rate journals such as the *Quarterly Journal of Economics*, the *Review of Economic Studies* and the *Economic Journal*. In a nutshell the Capital Theory Controversies highlighted the logical problems inherent in the concept of aggregate capital, thus undermining the aggregate version of the Neoclassical theories of growth and income distribution. One of the major contributions to the controversies was Sraffa's demonstration that a set of commodity prices could be derived based on the technical conditions of production without any marginalist analysis, and with no concept of aggregate capital (Sraffa 1960). Moreover, together with the issue of competing ideologies and visions of economics, the Controversies highlighted the problem of using equilibrium analysis as a tool for analysing processes of capital accumulation and growth. Here the debate was about the legitimacy of using comparative static exercises, i.e. differences in the parameters of an equilibrium model, for the analysis of economic processes, namely the effects of changes taking place over time. As Robinson explained, the former analysis is able to answer 'what-would-be-different-if' type of questions, whereas the latter is concerned with 'what-would-follow-if' type of questions (Robinson 1974).

The Capital Theory Controversies provided a renewed sense of identity for those Keynesians who considered Keynes's writings to be a move beyond marginalist theorising (Mata 2004). Socio-economic conditions also played a role. The end of the long post-war boom and the apparent inability of standard Keynesian theory and policy to deal with stagflation undermined the Neoclassical synthesis (but see Seidman 2003). Mainstream economic theory responded initially by developing New Classical macro-economic models explicitly based on optimising microfoundations with rational expectations and continuous market clearing. These New Classical models rejected demand-side policies to control the growing levels of unemployment in the industrialised economies and advocated the need for supply-side measures, especially labour market reforms to increase wage flexibility. All of these factors combined to give an added urgency to the imperative for non-mainstream economists to develop an alternative economic theory based on more realistic microfoundations. The result was the emergence of a distinct Post Keynesian school of thought, recognised as such by both mainstream and non-mainstream economists.

The romantic age: the search for a grand theoretical system

The main unifying theme of Post Keynesian economics as it emerged was the need to replace Neoclassical economics with a radical alternative based on the recovery of Keynes's original insights. In the Richard Ely Lecture at the 1972 New Orleans meeting of the American Economics Association, Joan Robinson talked of a second crisis in economics (Robinson 1972). To her, the Great Depression together with the failure of Neoclassical economics to provide a solution to low income and large unemployment led to a first crisis of conventional economic theory. Out of this crisis emerged the so-called Keynesian revolution. Keynes became the accepted orthodoxy, and the use of government expenditure for stabilisation purposes, whatever the purpose of it, the unquestionable rule to achieve and maintain full employment. Prosperity seemed to follow everywhere in the industrialised (broadly OECD) countries in what has been variously called 'the long boom' or 'the Keynesian golden age' (circa 1948–1973).

However, from the early 1970s many of the real-world's economies were suffering from significant economic problems, namely rising inflation, an increase in third-world poverty, pollution and wasteful armaments expenditure. Joan Robinson complained that, for the second time in history, conventional economic theory had nothing to say on the most urgent problems of the time. For Robinson, on this occasion, the problems arose mainly from a simple but major omission. Orthodox Keynesian economists had omitted to discuss what the objective of a higher level of employment should be, i.e. more balanced income distribution and higher growth. According to Robinson, orthodox Keynesians lacked a sound theory of distribution and growth (Robinson 1972: 8). An enthusiastic audience greeted the Lecture. As a result of it, Robinson was encouraged to write an economic textbook aimed at introducing Post Keynesian economics to young economists (Robinson and Eatwell 1973).

In the USA, Robinson had found energetic support in Sidney Weintraub, who by the early 1960s had already made important contributions to the theories of aggregate supply, distribution and inflation (e.g. Weintraub 1958, 1959). In the 1970s, Weintraub voiced his opposition to Neoclassical economics, and established himself as one of most strenuous defenders of tax-based income policy (e.g. Wallich and Weintraub 1971). Some of these ideas were further developed by his student Paul Davidson (e.g. Davidson and Smolensky 1964), who went on to become one of the most influential representatives of Post Keynesian economics, especially of its monetary strand (e.g. Davidson 1965, 1972). Monetary and financial issues were also at the heart of Hyman Minsky's contributions, later crystallised in the financial fragility hypothesis (e.g. Minsky 1975, 1977; see, for the modern legacy of Minsky's work, Bellofiore and Ferri 2001). As a member of the younger American generation, Jan Kregel was crucial in attempting to integrate Keynes's monetary analysis with Cambridge contributions on growth and distribution. However, he soon lamented the lack of a Post Keynesian theory of price formation in corporate capitalism (e.g. Kregel 1973: 207). The problem was short-lived as this was to be the main area of Alfred Eichner's contributions (e.g. Eichner 1973), eventually leading to the celebrated theory of the megacorp (Eichner 1976).[3]

Despite this diversity of contributions, Post Keynesian economics was believed to have an essential unity of theoretical purpose, with the potential for becoming a comprehensive alternative to the dominant Neoclassical paradigm (Eichner and Kregel 1975: 1294; see also Eichner 1979). Post Keynesian economics was seen as a well-defined approach making a distinct theoretical and practical contribution to the understanding of real-world problems. The research objective was to create a grand Post Keynesian theoretical system that could match the comprehensiveness of Neoclassical theory (Pasinetti 1974). In this sense Post Keynesian economics was an attempt to take on the mainstream paradigm on its own terms. Eichner and Kregel (1975) distinguished four characteristic features of the new Post Keynesian paradigm:

3 Other Post Keynesian contributions on price theory in corporate capitalism include Wood (1975), and Harcourt and Kenyon (1976).

1   a dynamic theory of growth based on historical rather than logical time;
2   an explanation of the distribution of income strictly related to the rate
     of economic expansion;
3   a credit theory of investment;
4   a microeconomic perspective grounded on imperfect markets with
     significant monopolistic elements.

The four characteristic features of Post Keynesian economics were claimed to represent a theoretical advance on Neoclassical economics. Post Keynesian economics was seen to offer a set of new theoretical tools that were more appropriate for the study of, and the solution to, real-world problems. The growth and increasing confidence of Post Keynesian economists initiated and fostered the development of a social and institutional framework to promote the new body of ideas (Lee 1995, 2000), including the launch of new academic journals such as the *Cambridge Journal of Economics* (1977) and the *Journal of Post Keynesian Economics* (1978).

In retrospect, a serious shortcoming of Post Keynesian economics during the period of optimism and excitement that characterised what we might call the romantic age of the 1970s was the almost exclusive concern with the theoretical structure of the Neoclassical paradigm. Most Post Keynesians considered the rejection of Neoclassical economics to be primarily a matter of theoretical differences. Post Keynesians advocated the replacement of the optimisation calculus with more realistic behavioural assumptions, such as imperfect competition, mark-up pricing and capacity-expanding investments (i.e. the accelerator model). However, the overriding emphasis on the theoretical critique of Neoclassical economics was not universally supported. One of the principal exponents of the need for a more thorough critique, not just at the theoretical level, but also at the methodological level, was, again, Joan Robinson, who recognised the dangers of trying to replace one closed theoretical system with another such system (Robinson 1979: 119).

The Post Keynesian critique of Neoclassical economics thus soon led to a recognition that at the root of most of the theoretical disputes lay profound differences in methodologies. The end of the romantic age in the early 1980s was marked by an increasing awareness of the importance of the characteristic methodological features of Post Keynesian economics. The new Post Keynesian paradigm was still viewed as possessing the potential to become an alternative to the Neoclassical paradigm, but the transformation came to be seen as much more fundamental than initially envisaged. Post Keynesian economics had become an alternative theoretical and methodological approach to Neoclassical economics. At the same time, the increasing concern with the methodological originality of Post Keynesian economics served to exacerbate the disputes between and within the different strands of Post Keynesian economics. The treatment of money, time and uncertainty became a key issue in these disputes. The romantic age gave way to what we might call the age of uncertainty.

The age of uncertainty: the search for an alternative methodology

The optimism and excitement of the romantic age and the search for a grand theoretical system to replace Neoclassical economics has been followed by a period of doubt and deep internal tensions within Post Keynesian economics. Post Keynesian economists have become increasingly concerned with the failure to transform the discipline of economics. Their contributions were either ignored or considered irrelevant. The growing self-doubt in Post Keynesian economics started with a preoccupation with the 'true' meaning of Keynes's theory. For example, the annotated bibliography of Post Keynesian economics lists 248 entries on 'interpretations of Keynes' up to 1994 of which more than half were between 1980 and 1990 (King 1995: Ch. E). The period of self-doubt then gave rise to the emergence of a greater diversity of alternative theoretical perspectives. The index of the recently published *Companion to Post Keynesian Economics* contains, for example, several streams of Post Keynesian thinking, including entries on Fundamentalist Keynesians, Institutionalism, Joan Robinson's economics, Kaldorian economics, Kaleckian economics, Monetary Circuit theory and Sraffian/Neo-Ricardian economics (King 2003). This greater diversity of alternative theoretical perspectives has tended to undermine the Post Keynesian claim to provide an alternative and coherent theoretical framework. Ultimately, the greater diversity has sparked off the search for the appropriate specification of the methodology of diversity, and led to the question of what the future of Post Keynesian economics will be (e.g. Walters and Young 1997). Despite recent attempts to elaborate new economic theories and policies, doubts and deep internal tensions about the direction of future research continue today.

The age of uncertainty can be traced back to internal and external circumstances. As for the former, most prominent are the disputes that arose with the emergence of the Neo-Ricardian approach in the late 1970s and early 1980s. Neo-Ricardian economists like Garegnani (1978, 1979), Eatwell (1979) and Milgate (1982) sought to create a grand theoretical system from a synthesis of Sraffa's model of prices and Keynes's principle of effective demand. The characteristic feature of the Neo-Ricardian theoretical system is the clear separation between the different mechanisms determining prices and quantities of goods and services in the economy. This is in contrast to the simultaneous determination of equilibrium prices and quantities in the

Neoclassical system. This Neo-Ricardian approach followed early Classical economics in adopting a long-period method of analysis, a static equilibrium approach set in logical (not historical) time, and focusing on the 'centre of gravitation' of the economic system associated with the dominant economic forces. In its most extreme form, the Neo-Ricardian approach rejected the importance of money, time and uncertainty in Keynes's analysis (however see, for a more conciliatory view, Roncaglia 1978). The analysis of long-term expectations and liquidity preference by Keynes was interpreted as mainstream imperfectionist arguments that arose out of his retention of Neoclassical marginal productivity theory, particularly the marginal efficiency of capital (Milgate 1982).

The Neo-Ricardian dismissal of Keynes's theories of money and behaviour under uncertainty coupled with the use of static equilibrium methods was in direct conflict with the Non-ergodic/Monetary Post Keynesian view of economists like Robinson, Shackle, Davidson and Chick. These prominent Post Keynesians argued for the fundamental importance of Keynes's analysis of money, time and uncertainty and the need for a more dynamic historical-time method of analysis (Fontana and Gerrard 1999). From this perspective, at least in its most extreme form, the Neo-Ricardian analysis represented the continuation of the Classical methods of analysis, albeit underpinning a non-Neoclassical theoretical structure. Similar tensions also arose between the Non-ergodic/Monetary strand and the Kaleckian strand. Again, from the Non-ergodic/Monetary perspective, the Kaleckian approach attaches too little significance to the effects of uncertainty, and instead it concentrates on developing deterministic equilibrium models based on non-Neoclassical microfoundations (however see, for a more conciliatory view, Sawyer 2001a).[4]

There are also important external circumstances which explain the growing self-doubts among Post Keynesian economists. First, there was the question of the significance of the result of the Capital Theory Controversies. Most Post Keynesian economists truly believed that the Controversies had called for a paradigm shift. They were thus puzzled by the tenacity of mainstream economists in ignoring the relevance of the critique of aggregate production functions. Second, there was the issue of the gradual exclusion of Post Keynesian economists from publishing in leading journals. Editors and referees pointed to the lack of formalisation

---

4   For instance, Sawyer (1985, 2001a) argues that Kalecki's approach dismissed equilibrium analysis, and his theory of effective demand was always set in the context of economic cycles. Sawyer also maintains that Kalecki and Kaleckian analyses always incorporate the endogenous money hypothesis (see Chapter 6, below), if only implicitly, whereas this is not always the case for many Post Keynesian analyses.

in Post Keynesian economics, and this naturally led to the complicated methodological question of what is 'proper' economics. Finally, in 1971 the Royal Economic Society had begun to publish *The Collected Writings of John Maynard*. Consequently material not previously accessible became easily available and material published in obscure outlets became easily available to a large audience. These publications prompted a major shift in Post Keynesian research, away from economic theory and policy and towards philosophy and methodology (e.g. Lawson 1985, Fitzgibbons 1988, Carabelli 1988 and O'Donnell 1989).

The tension between the Neo-Ricardian and the Non-ergodic/Monetary streams of Post Keynesian economics, together with the above-discussed external sources of problems has had two important consequences. First, as stated above, there has been a proliferation of alternative Post Keynesian analyses. For many scholars, diversity is now a defining characteristic of Post Keynesian economics. This was the conclusion of Hamouda and Harcourt (1989) in their survey of Post Keynesian economics, where they maintained that there was no uniform way of tackling all issues in economics. Post Keynesian analyses differed from one another not least because they were concerned with different issues, and often used different levels of abstraction. Post Keynesian economics should thus be seen as a portmanteau term describing the work of a very heterogeneous group of economists, united by a rejection of Neoclassical economics (see also Backhouse 1998) and seeking to provide an alternative paradigm. In a similar vein, Sawyer (1991) and more recently Arestis *et al.* (1999) have argued that the vigour of Post Keynesian research derives from the pluralism of theories, methods and assumptions (see also Harcourt 1998, 1999).

Second, and partly related to the emergence of these alternative theoretical perspectives, there has been a growing concern with the methodological features of Post Keynesian economics (e.g. Chick 1995a, Dow 1995a, 2002; but see, for early methodological claims, Chick 1983). This search for a methodology consistent with Post Keynesian economics has, at least initially, proceeded in terms of a critique of Neoclassical methodology.[5] As Lawson points out, Neoclassical economics is ultimately defined by its methodology, and hence any non-Neoclassical alternative must also be defined by an alternative non-Neoclassical methodology (Lawson 1999: 7). From this perspective, the diversity of methods of analysis is an important methodological principle of Post Keynesian economics. In other words, the

---

5 A noteworthy exception is Dow (e.g. 1996c), where the search for a Post Keynesian methodology proceeds in terms of an analysis of the distinct methodologies, which implicitly or explicitly underpin the different schools of thought in economics.

methodology of diversity has become a core characteristic of Post Keynesian economics (Dow 1992: 111).

Drawing on the work of Lawson (1997), Downward and Mearman (2002) have explained that Neoclassical theory embraces a deductive method of explanation based on the intrinsic and extrinsic conditions of closure (ICC and ECC, respectively). The ICC implies that a cause always produces the same effect, whereas the ECC implies that an effect always has the same cause. It follows that Neoclassical theory implicitly assumes that the structure of the phenomenon under observation is constant, and that it is possible to isolate the actual cause of changes from other potential influences. These features are considered at odds with the Post Keynesian research programme. In particular, the Neoclassical method of explanation is considered incompatible with the variety of Post Keynesian theories and methods of analysis. The emerging consensus is that critical realism provides the organising methodological principle for Post Keynesian economics (Lawson 1994, 1999, 2003a).[6]

According to this alternative methodology, reality is made up of complex interactions of facts and events (actual reality), experience and impression (empirical reality), and structures and mechanisms that order events (non-actual reality). In other words, there is a material and social world that must be investigated independently of its appearance and perception. The perspective of the research is thus not on facts and their relations, but on mechanisms and tendencies that regulate those facts. The social theory supported by critical realism recognises individuals in their social environment as the heart of the economic analysis (organicism). Social entities such as groups or institutions are concrete things as well as 'abstract models'. Weber's *Verstehen* notion is relevant here, because social reality and agents' actions are mediated by the subjective process of attaching meaning to reality. Nevertheless, Weber's notion must be interpreted in the restrictive sense that economists should develop an understanding of the frame of reference within which groups of individuals take decisions. Individuals are defined according to their functions in the economic process: production (entrepreneurs), work and consumption (households) and credit creation (bankers). Thus, analysis should pay attention to the choices of groups of individuals, rather than to individual choices. In other words, how individuals make sense of the world is determined by the role that they play in the economic process. Since reality is a network of objective structures

6   See Brown *et al.* (2002), and Critical Realism (1999, 2002) for an assessment of the critical realism stance regarding the way economic theorising and empirical work should be carried out in broadly defined Post Keynesian economics.

and subjective interpretations of facts, methodology is necessary to make explicit beliefs and presuppositions used by scholars to justify their theories. Consequently, the method of inference must rely upon a continuous movement from the conception of the object analysed to the conception of the structure and mechanisms that explain that object. Retroduction or abduction is the term for this movement, mediated by our perception, from the actual reality to the non-actual reality (Lawson 2003a).

Critical realism is considered the appropriate method of explanation for Post Keynesian economics, because it renders the latter intelligible in its essential features, though this book favours a particular interpretation of it, namely the encompassing view. Critical realism emphasises the need for open-system theorising to provide realistic causal explanations that recognise the complexity of the social and institutional context of behaviour. Critical realism explicitly draws attention to the diverse structures and mechanisms that regulate modern economies, and in so doing, lends support to the variety of alternative theoretical analyses that come under the umbrella of Post Keynesian economics. It suggests that the appropriate epistemological goal for economics should be to identify the causality of actual events by investigating real causal structures that may be stable (and, hence, capable of being stated as causal 'laws'), but not inherently predictable (Dow 1999). It also argues for the use of multiple tools of explanatory analysis. Interviews or case studies can help to establish context-specific understanding, while mathematical and statistical methods can help identify more general causal regularities (Downward and Mearman 2002).

The encompassing view is a particular interpretation of critical realism.[7] This view recognises the critical realist commitment to open-system theorising, but it defends a positive outlook towards Neoclassical economics. The encompassing view does question, as Keynes did, the universal relevance of Neoclassical economics, but it also rejects the view that it is *a priori* universally irrelevant. For this reason, the encompassing view suggests a two-stage analysis. First, Post Keynesian economists should aim to identify the limits to the domains of relevance of existing theoretical models. Second, they should plan on developing more general models that encompass the existing models in a synthesis with new models in order to extend the domains of relevance (Fontana and Gerrard 2002a, see also Gerrard 1989, 1991, 1992b, Chick 1995b: 30–34).

Therefore, whereas the encompassing principle should help to explain diversity and conflict between different Post Keynesian strands, it should

---

7 See Pratten (2005) for a lucid exposition of the progressive aspects of the critical realism research programme.

also facilitate and encourage investigations outside Post Keynesian economics, thus having the potential to help bridge the gap between different economic traditions. In this sense, the encompassing principle acts as a ground-clearing device for opening the debate between different approaches to economics (Lawson 1994, Arestis 1996). It offers the chance for a dialogue between different economic approaches and for this reason, in this book, is the preferred mode of reproduction for dissent in Post Keynesian economics

Conclusions

This brief survey of the historical development of Post Keynesian economics confirms that the Post Keynesian mode for expressing Keynesian dissent is usually expressed at the level of first principles. It is an engagement with the basic structure of the theory and the methodology of economic analysis. As for the theory, the emerging consensus is that the three pillars that should inform the theoretical dissent in Post Keynesian economics are related to three broad topics, namely uncertainty, money and time. This explains the title of this book and its aim to provide a coherent framework for assessing recent contributions in those three major research areas.

As for the methodology of Post Keynesian analysis, this chapter supports the view that critical realism is the appropriate methodology for Post Keynesian economics, though it favours a particular interpretation of it, namely the encompassing view.

3 Methodology and economic theory in Keynes's *General Theory*

Introduction

More than three decades ago Clower and Leijonhufvud (1975) wrote a joint paper to address the central message of Keynes's *The General Theory of Employment, Interest and Money* (1936). They start the paper by complaining about the infinite regress on the meaning of the work of Keynes. They maintain that the debate on what Keynes meant will never be settled, though no explanation is provided for their view,[1] and they prefer instead to take a critical look at the main features of a typical Keynesian model. But then, with considerable candour, they acknowledge that the state of affairs from this perspective is no more comforting. To state the case succinctly, Clower and Leijonhufvud argue that the typical Keynesian model, such as the *IS-LM* model, imposes virtually no analytical discipline upon its users (Clower and Leijonhufvud 1975: 182). They speculate that addressing the way individual economic agents co-ordinate production, consumption and trading activities is a possible way to impose some useful constraints upon the construction of a Keynesian model.

This chapter offers a different interpretation of the current situation in Keynesian economics. Keynes is usually interpreted as proposing, or intending to propose, an original theory of employment and income (Keynes 1935a). However, Keynes saw himself breaking away from Classical orthodoxy at the connected levels of theory and methods. In fact, Keynes used the term 'orthodoxy' or 'classical theory' to indicate the economic tradition from Smith and Ricardo through to Marshall and Pigou. This is

---

1 Gerrard explains that interpretations are by their very nature creative acts of readers. More precisely, the perceived meaning of the text is affected by, and affects, the different contexts in which readers read the text (Gerrard 1991). Thus, at least some of the interpretative controversies surrounding the writings of Keynes are due to contextual differences.

apparently a rather confusing description. Conventionally, Classical economics is the term used to describe the economic theory of the period from Adam Smith to the marginalist revolution. But Keynes perceived that what he was really attacking was more than a theoretical tradition. It was the continuity at the level of hypotheses, presuppositions and methods. Keynes's 'Classics' were thus the theories and the methods of Smith and Ricardo as well as his Neoclassical followers (Hicks 1967a: 155, Gerrard 1995: 446).

Hicks was successful in presenting Keynes's theory at the Oxford meeting of the Econometric Society (see also Meade 1936–37, Harrod 1937), and 'Mr Keynes and the "Classics"' (Hicks 1937) established what Clower and Leijonhufvud have called the standard view of the Keynesian model (see also Young 1987, Darity and Young 1995). However, as Hicks later recognised, theoretical analysis is only part of the story of the relationship between Keynes and the 'Classics' (Ambrosi 2004). They were indeed saying different things. But how, and why, did Keynes and the 'Classics' say these different things? Several economists, including Clower and Leijonhufvud, have attempted to answer these questions. However, these attempts have focused exclusively on theoretical differences between Keynes and the 'Classics'. This chapter takes a different view, and argues for a more general approach, which highlights the role of methods, in addition to theories, in order to explain the particular nature of Keynes's work. The suggestion is that the methodological differences between Keynes and the 'Classics' are relevant, at least in part, in explaining the unrestricted analytical licence of the Keynesian model. Furthermore, economists going back to the old story of the relationship between Keynes and the 'Classics' can learn something about controversial issues surrounding the modern debate on the roles of formalism and experiments in economics (Downward and Mearman 2002).

Keynes's method: Chapter 18 of the *General Theory*

In Chapter 18 of the *General Theory*, Keynes restates his theory of employment in the form of a simple model. He lists the main economic factors as dependent variables, independent variables and given factors. As for the given factors, Keynes explains that they share the same nature as independent variables but, in the place and context of the research, they can be considered as having negligible effects on the dependent variables. The dependent variables are the volume of employment and the national income. The independent variables are the wage-unit, the supply of money and three fundamental psychological factors, namely the propensity to consume, the attitude towards liquidity and the expectations of future yield from capital assets.[2] The given factors are the skill and quantity of labour, the quality and quantity of equipment, the existing technique, the degree of competition, the tastes and habits of consumers, the disutility of different intensities of labour and the social structure (Keynes 1936: 245).

Several authors have made reference to Chapter 18 in order to evaluate the originality of the contribution of Keynes as compared to pre-Keynesian analyses of unemployment (see, for example, Greenwald and Stiglitz 1987: 121(3)). Without denying the value of these investigations, these authors often tend to blur the distinction between the different levels of Keynes's work. Keynes made original contributions at both the theoretical and methodological levels, and it is important that those two levels be considered together in any evaluation of the exact nature of his contribution to economics (Dow 1984: 5, Gerrard 1997: 166). The problem is not simply that there are real differences between Keynesian economics and the economics of Keynes (Leijonhufvud 1968), but rather that the latter takes on completely different meanings depending on the methodological stance used to interpret it. In Keynes's writings, theory and method have, in a very significant way, an interdependent existence. For instance, some commentators have appreciated that problems of money and expectations were the main concerns for Keynes, as they are now for current macroeconomists, and yet they have maintained his theoretical project was a disastrous failure (see, for example, Kohn 1986: 1219).[3] Unfortunately, this type of interpretation fails to understand that his original theory rests on a methodology completely different from that of the Neoclassical economists (Dow 1995b). Thus, what appears to be a disastrous failure to a Neoclassical economist may be seen as strength by a close follower of Keynes. Failure is a rather slippery concept, because failure or success in a project depends very much upon what it is intended to achieve, and that rests on the methodological foundations of the theory to which that project aims to contribute.

An implicit assumption of conventional interpretations is that Keynes adopted the methodology of Classical economists. As was explained in Chapter 2, the aim of Classical methodology is to discover or confirm invariant laws or universal principles that govern real-world facts or events (Lawson 1997). Reality is seen as being approximated by a system defined by intrinsic and extrinsic conditions of closure. The former assumes that the

---

2 However, Keynes warns that these independent variables 'would be capable of being subjected to further analysis, and are not, so to speak, our ultimate atomic independent elements' (Keynes 1936: 246–247).

3 In the specific, Kohn argues that Keynes failed to establish the primacy of monetary analysis over the real analysis of Classical economists.

structure of the phenomenon under observation is constant; hence a cause always produces the same effect. The latter assumes the possibility of isolating the actual cause of an event from other potential contributing causes It is a complement to the intrinsic condition of closure in the sense that it implies that an effect is the exclusive outcome of a sole cause. From this methodological perspective, the contribution of Keynes consisted of asking awkward questions, and discussing problems related to specific areas of Classical theory (e.g. unemployment theory). It was an internal critique of the conventional theory. Keynes had raised important issues that were effectively, though often slowly, translated into new variables or coefficients for Classical models. Few questioned whether these issues could actually be discussed, let alone solved, within the conventional framework. It is worth noting that the claim that the distinctiveness of Keynes's theory and methodology was not sufficiently appreciated has a long, though poorly understood, tradition that can be traced back to his young colleagues and followers:

> The lack of appreciation by some of the older school of economics may have followed naturally from their method of approach. They turned over his pages in a somewhat critical spirit, seeking aspects of the truth which they had neglected. They found that Keynes made certain points very effectively. He stressed the importance of expectation in determining present values. Yes; this was a point which had always been in their minds, but which he was probably quite right in saying that they had not stressed sufficiently. A mental note was made. Then again, there was his elaborate analysis of liquidity preference. Here certainly was something interesting. Reference to what he had in mind had sometimes been made in the discussion of velocity of circulation. But he was certainly right in holding that all this should be much more heavily stressed. These points might be jotted down for incorporation in the relevant sections of next year's lecture notes.
>
> (Harrod 1951: 463–464, see also Robinson 1979: 119)

The principal novelties of Keynes seemed to be the theory of expectations and liquidity preference. The next task was to see what the implications of these theoretical innovations were, and how traditional models could incorporate them. There are obvious theoretical and empirical reasons for adopting such an approach. In fact, it is quite reasonable that new ideas are first interpreted in the light of the existing set of models. However, as time goes on, it is increasingly evident that conventional models have limited ability to explain important economic phenomena to which Keynes devoted much thought (Fontana and Gerrard 2006).

Among the most interesting, and yet least studied, issues in economic theory (Akerlof 2002) are the problem of the fundamentally mutable nature of expectations under conditions of ambiguity and uncertainty (Fontana and Gerrard 1999, Starmer 1999) and the roles of custom, convention and institutions – for example, contracts and money – as a way of coping with these conditions (Palley 1996c, Howitt 1997, Fontana 2000, Downward *et al.* 2002). It is the contention of this book that the limitations of modern conventional models are no different in nature from the critical issues voiced by Keynes against Classical theory (see, for example, Keynes 1937). These limitations are indicative of the relevance of an analytical project that aims to reassess Keynes's legacy in the light of a closer relationship between theory and method.

From this perspective, Chapter 18 represents much more than the summary of a theory of employment and output. It restates an innovative theory of employment and income, together with the original methodology upon which it is based. In that chapter, Keynes emphasises two interconnected levels of his research, namely 'the logical necessity of the model' and 'the safe generalisations from experience'. By the logical necessity of the model, Keynes refers to the different roles that economic factors play in explaining the extreme complexity of modern economic problems. It is a reference to what is possible in principle. What, for example, are the *logically necessary* effects of an increase or decrease in the rate of investment? Or, similarly, how exactly does the rate of consumption vary when income changes? A set of fully specified equations with an equal number of unknowns provides a clear and definite answer to these questions. In this sense, Keynes can be interpreted as offering an alternative set of equations to the Classical theory. However, Keynes also suggests that although the independent variables can take on any value, they *actually* tend to take on only a few particular values. These values are not logically necessary, but they are safe generalisations from experience. Here the suggestion is that important knowledge can be acquired with partial and incomplete formulations (Brunner 1986: 60).

Carabelli (1988: Ch. 8) and Gerrard (1992a) offer much in the way of textual evidence supporting the view that Keynes considered 'the logical necessity of the model' and 'the safe generalisations from experience' as interconnected levels of his research. In particular, Gerrard (1992a: 4–7) considers Keynes's mature writings in the light of the essay 'My early beliefs', written for the Bloomsbury Memoir Club in September 1938. Gerrard shows that in retrospect Keynes saw his early philosophical beliefs as too formalistic, too faithful to the idea of attaining knowledge that was certain, complete and precise. More to the point, in his 1931 review of Ramsey's *The Foundations of Mathematics*, Keynes embraced the distinction between formal logic and human logic (Keynes 1931: 338–339).

Whereas the former was exclusively concerned with the rules of consistent thought, the latter had a more general character as it included the study of useful mental habits. As argued in the next chapter, Keynes used this different interpretation of the nature and functions of logic in his economic writings, especially in the *General Theory*. There, more than in any other case, he recognised the organic nature of economic material, and the consequent vagueness of human knowledge. His new theory was then coupled with an original methodology that did not reject formalism, but recommended complementing it with experience and empirical practices. The final outcome of his equilibrium analysis of employment is thus a temporary, but continually shifting, communion between formal analysis and general experience (see Chick and Dow 2001: 713; also Chick and Caserta 1997).

Chapter 18 of the *General Theory* is thus an important example of Keynes's way of thinking about economic reality (see, for a similar argument, Shackle 1967: 158, Sardoni 1989: 294; also Harcourt 1992). It invites readers to rediscover the interdependence between theory and method. It alludes to his concern for an alternative framework to the theory and the methodology of Classical economists.

Keynes versus the 'Classics': scope and method of economics

According to Keynes, economics evolved as new concepts were proposed to explain and understand real economic events (Carabelli 1988: 157–159). Explanation consisted essentially of representations and descriptions of actual facts. Explanation was important, but it was necessarily directed to, and limited by, the evidence available. In fact, understanding was the natural complement to the activity of explanation. Understanding referred to the interpretation of the underlying mechanisms and tendencies, the laws of action in Keynes's own words, which governed the observed economic events. Keynes soon realised that Classical economics needed to be rescued at both levels. For this purpose, he made a distinction between explanations based on partial and general experiences (see, for example, his approval of Malthus's view on the relationship between experience and theory, Keynes 1935b: 108). Similarly, he distinguished between the search for permanent and provisional laws of motion of economic events (Keynes 1938b: 299–300).

Whereas Keynes accepted that the aim of economic analysis was to represent and describe real events, he cautioned that what was available as relevant evidence was necessarily a matter of interpretation. In order to construct any theory, economists have to abstract from the complexities of reality, and there are different ways of carrying out that process. According to Keynes, there was a significant flaw in the process of abstraction by (late) Classical economists. They had ignored important features of modern monetary economies. More precisely, they had omitted from their process of abstraction the conditions that could explain the emergence of economic crises (Keynes 1933a: 411).

How could Classical economists have proposed a valuable abstraction, and yet have excluded from the outset what were considered to be important features of the economic reality? How could they have made such a basic mistake? According to Keynes, there are two primary ways of conducting the process of abstraction (see, for similar arguments, Dobb 1937: 127–132, Lawson 1997: 227–237). First, an economist can represent reality in terms of a thought experiment, i.e. a theoretical laboratory to test new ideas. Classical models were excellent examples of this type of abstraction. But, he argued, there was a second way to carry out the process of abstraction. Through intimate and messy acquaintance with the historical facts and events under investigation, an economist could elaborate an original way of thinking about reality (Keynes 1938b: 299). Models could be seen as general instruments of thought, appreciative of the main characteristics of the object of analysis, but free from the assumption of universality in space and time.

By contrast, Classical economics models were used as fictional constructs. They assumed independence between the factors involved in the analysis. In this way, the representation of the economic system was open to all sorts of algebraic manipulations and elegant formalisation. What was wanted in this case was a way of determining how a laboratory system worked, if such a thing existed. Of course, at this stage theory was of little use in explaining the workings of real-world economics. The description of real events was not an issue. Theory could conflict with real-world practice. Indeed, Classical economists had accepted that their models were in the nature of an intellectual experiment, and yet they claimed that economic models were still of great practical importance. Classical economists could make this claim because they saw abstraction as a method of successive approximations (see, for a modern discussion of this method, Hahn 1973b: 136–137, Hicks 1983: 374). From their perspective, it was legitimate to ignore important features of reality. It was a useful first step to achieving their goal, namely a rigorous and formal representation of the economy. And, for this purpose, they needed what Carabelli calls the assumption of 'logical independence from' (Carabelli 1991: 114). As a result of this assumption, economic reality could be understood as approximating to a system governed by intrinsic and extrinsic conditions of closure. It was only after a single and stable mechanism equivalent to some observed events was uncovered that reality could play its role. Real and important features excluded from the first stage of the process of abstraction could then be confronted with theory. By using *ad hoc* assumptions, and introducing auxiliary hypotheses, theory could accommodate some critical evidence. In this way Classical economics was slowly transformed into an accurate theory. Keynes explained this was the case with the Classical theory of money (see, for example, Keynes 1933a: 410) and decision-making under conditions of uncertainty (see, for example, Keynes 1937: 112–113). But, could Classical economics really be amended in such a way as to reintroduce as a matter of analytical investigation what had been taken away at the very beginning? In other words, could Classical theory be extended to include more realistic features of modern economies without giving up its basic structure? Keynes clearly saw this possibility, and he did not spare his comments.

> One can make some quite worth while [*sic*] progress merely by using your axioms and maxims. But one cannot get very far except by devising new and improved models. This requires, as you say, 'a vigilant observation of the actual working of our system'. Progress in economics consists almost entirely in a progressive improvement in the choice of models. The grave fault of the later classical school, exemplified by Pigou, has been to *overwork a too simple or out-of-date model*, and in not seeing that progress lay in improving the model; whilst Marshall often confused his models, for devising which he had great genius, by wanting to be realistic and by being unnecessarily ashamed of lean and abstract outlines.
>
> (Keynes 1938a: 296, italics added)

Keynes strongly opposed the Classical method of abstraction. He repudiated the idea of creating a fictional theory and then making it more realistic by encompassing, step by step, important features of the real world. More importantly, he recognised that the Classical process of abstraction derived from, and was consistent with, a mode of explanation based on partial experience, and with the search for a permanent law of action governing economic events. Thus, in proposing an alternative to the Classical method of abstraction, Keynes actually suggested a different scope for economic enquiries. The representation and description of real events had to be based on general rather than partial experience. In the same way, he maintained that economists should search for provisional rather than permanent laws of action governing economic events.

Keynes saw devising new models rather than overworking the too simple classical model as being the way to progress in economics. With this in mind, he aimed to distance himself from both Pigou and Marshall. In respect of the former, and Classical economists more generally, he lamented drawing general inferences from a model that was based on a very confined practice.

This was a case of claiming general knowledge from very partial experience. As he explained, economic material, i.e. the object of analysis in economics, is non-homogeneous through time and, by extension, space, with the result that any model is historically and geographically determined. Thus, Classical economists had claimed more than it was possible to deliver (Keynes, 1937: 115). Having based their theory on very partial experience, Classical economists believed that they had succeeded in their search for a permanent law of action. However, this was the Classical fallacy. Economic reality is the complex outcome of several and unstable causal forces. It was pure illusion to pretend to uncover a single and stable law of motion once and for all out of that complexity. As he told the League of Nations when asked for a comment on two volumes by Tinbergen, '[i]s it assumed that the factors investigated are comprehensive and that they are not merely a partial selection out of all the factors at work? How much difference does it make to the method if they are not comprehensive?' (Keynes 1938c: 286–287). For Keynes, economics was concerned with motives, expectations and psychological uncertainties; hence the factors investigated could never be presumed to be comprehensive (e.g. Keynes 1938d: 295). Thus, compared to the Classical perspective, Keynes had a modest, but more realistic, view of what economics could possibly deliver. Economists had to aim to uncover the single mechanism governing the wide variety of events under investigation, but they had to be well aware of the precarious state of their analyses.[4] Novel partial experience could soon signal the prevalence of another, and yet unstable, law of action.

With regard to Marshall, Keynes deplored his resistance to general inferences. Keynes had great respect for the man whom he saw as the founder of Cambridge economics, but he was critical of Marshall's attitude to pure theory (Keynes 1933b: 199). Keynes accused Marshall of not being faithful to his own words. He speculated that Marshall may have been too anxious to establish economics as a social discipline with its own methods and purposes. For this reason, Marshall may have been content to play down

---

4   However, according to Keynes this low-key view of the nature of economic enquiries was, if anything, indicative of the complexity of the economic task. 'Professor Planck, of Berlin, the famous originator of the Quantum Theory, once remarked to me that in early life he had thought of studying economics, but had found it too difficult! Professor Planck could easily master the whole corpus of mathematical economics in a few days. He did not mean that! But the amalgam of logic and intuition and the wide knowledge of facts, most of which are not precise, which is required for economic interpretation in its highest form is, quite truly, overwhelmingly difficult for those whose gifts mainly consist in the power to imagine and pursue to their furthest points the implications and prior conditions of comparatively simple facts which are known with a high degree of precision' (Keynes 1933b: 186(2)).

the role of abstraction and general inferences, which he believed to be the conventional machinery of natural sciences.

From Marshall, Keynes accepted the particular nature of the economic enquiry. Unlike the standard case in natural sciences, economic material is not homogeneous through time, with the result that it is never possible to claim universality in space and time for any economic theory. At the same time, Keynes believed that economists had to assign a transcendental universality to their mode of thought. In this sense, economic models had to be considered as instruments of universal application for the discovery of a certain class of mechanisms or laws of action. For this purpose, models had to abstract from the 'concrete truth' of real-world events. They had to focus on the explanation and understanding of a wide variety of events, what Malthus called general experience as opposed to partial experience. This wide variety of facts and events may have consisted of the essential features of capitalist labour markets or the primary factors determining the money supply process in Britain at the beginning of the last century. Economic models had to be the engine for uncovering the underlying laws of action that had contributed to generate this variety of facts. It was a question of segmenting, partial segmenting to be sure, what were believed to be the main features of that general experience.

> Economics is a science of thinking in terms of models joined to the art of choosing models which are relevant to the contemporary world. . . . The object of a model is to segregate the semi-permanent or relatively constant factors from those which are transitory or fluctuating so as to develop a logical way of thinking about the latter, and of understanding the time sequences to which they give rise in particular cases.
>
> (Keynes 1938a: 296)

Keynes saw economic agents as creative individuals who learn and innovate. For this reason, economists are required to make use of introspection and personal judgement to weigh the role of expectations, motives and psychological uncertainties in explaining real-world events. From a practical point of view then, economic models have to change as reality changes.

Mr Keynes and the 'Classics' in prospect

Seven decades have elapsed since the publication of Keynes's *General Theory* and Hicks's 'Mr Keynes and the "Classics"'. In the interim, numerous scholars have been debating the central message of Keynes's works. What did Keynes say or mean? What can be retained, and possibly developed, out of his writings? Of course, there are so many differences between the economic system of his time and that of the modern world, that it would be naive to hope to find concrete solutions to current problems in his writings. However, as Chick argues, a rich methodology is one of the most robust creations of Keynes (Chick 1983: 12). By understanding his methods, modern scholars have the possibility of applying his reasoning to changed historical circumstances, and to adapt it to events not yet foreseen (see, for instance, Harcourt 2004). This book subscribes to that view. In particular, this chapter maintains that the methodological position of Keynes as recorded in his debate with the 'Classics' can inform the current debate in modern economics on two important issues: (a) the role of formalism, and (b) the role of experiments in economics.

In recent years, there has been an increasing interest in the role of formalism in economics, especially in Keynesian economics (e.g. Dow 1998). The standard line of argument is that Keynes rejected formalism. He was prevented from making use of symbolic representation, mathematics, statistical inferences and econometrics by the very nature of topical issues such as uncertainty and psychological factors, to which he attached great importance (O'Donnell 1997: 132–133). Recently, this same line of argument has been employed by economists critical of Post Keynesian economics (e.g. Walters and Young 1997). According to these critics, for the sake of consistency with the teachings of their master, Post Keynesian economists should avoid using quantitative methods like econometrics, since the economic material is not amenable to formal analyses.

As argued in the previous sections, there are serious doubts about the historical validity and the practical implications of this traditional line of argument. Classical economists described reality as approximating to a system defined by intrinsic and extrinsic conditions of closure. They saw formal methods as an unambiguous advance in the search for a universal law of motion governing a large variety of historical and geographical events. Keynes resisted this extensive use of formalism. He believed that economic knowledge is necessarily incomplete and partial. This incompleteness is inevitable as it is related to the continuously changing nature of real-world economies. In his view, economics was a branch of logic, a moral science rather than a natural science. It dealt with psychological values and expectations. At the same time, Keynes accepted that formalism had a useful role in economics. Rigour, precision and demonstrable results were seen as beneficial effects of using formal methods. It was in the nature of economic thinking to apply formal principles of thought (Keynes 1936: 297). Thus, his rather complex position was to endorse formalism cautiously. From this standpoint, Post Keynesian economists should not be afraid of using formal methods. The cautious approach to formalism in economics arises from an original theory and methodology that explicitly recognises agents as creative decision-makers.

At the same time, Keynes also emphasised the role of contracts, rules, habits and institutions as decision-making apparatuses evolving through time. He considered these tools to be a way of coping with the inherent uncertainty of individual decision-making. These tools provide and reflect stable, though temporary, conditions upon which economic agents can base their own behaviour. As such, these stable conditions lend themselves to formal methods of analysis (see, for example, Chick and Dow 2001: 714, Downward *et al.* 2002). In other words, the evolutionary nature of the economic material does not preclude the use of formal methods in economics, though it does call for an intimate relationship between theory and practice. It is significant that Keynes concluded his centenary allocution on Malthus (Keynes 1935b) by praising the original methodology of his predecessor, namely a combination of inductive arguments and formal thought (Keynes 1935b: 108). In practice, Keynes aimed to move beyond the Classical search for permanent laws of motion, towards making provisional inferences drawn from general experience. For this purpose, he endorsed the cautious use of formal methods in economics. This position represents a positive approach to formalism, and it should help to establish a more constructive role for formal methods in Post Keynesian economics.

Another important issue in modern economics is the role of experiments and behavioural analyses. As explained by Akerlof on the occasion of the award of the 2002 Nobel Prize in economics, psychological and sociological factors such as cognitive bias, reciprocity and fairness are central to economics, in particular to macroeconomic research programmes undertaken in the spirit of Keynes's *General Theory*. However, he complains that the '*ad hockery*' of the Neoclassical synthesis and its further development have overridden the role of psychological and sociological factors in economics (Akerlof 2002).

Recent developments in psychology and experimental economics seem to offer novel arguments for revisiting some of the most original aspects of Keynes's work (Fontana and Gerrard 2004). In particular, the heuristic and biases approach of Tversky and Kahneman (1974) has shown the relevance of psychological and sociological factors to understanding the cognitive processes that produce valid and invalid judgements in decision-making. The point of departure for the heuristic and biases approach is that individuals, in attempting to form intuitive predictions and judgements of uncertain events, are often influenced by what is similar (representativeness), comes easily to mind (availability) or comes first (anchoring). These heuristics are very useful tools for individuals making decisions under conditions of uncertainty, but they often lead to errors and biases. Tversky and Kahneman have undertaken an extensive analysis of these heuristics, and the consequent violations of standard economic analysis such as expected utility theory

(EUT). They have concluded that the presence of errors and biases reduces the usefulness of standard theory as a general descriptive model of human behaviour.

Against this background, the common economic interpretation of the heuristic and biases approach is to consider it to be the psychology of irrationality (e.g. Binmore 1999). Observed biases are viewed as examples of the non-rational aspects of human behaviour. These biases are seen as providing no general information about human behaviour. They are dramatic but rare exceptions to the predictions of standard economic theory and, as such, are not deemed to be of serious concern to economists. Most experimental economists find it difficult to explain this type of attitude. As Starmer says,

> mountains of experimental evidence reveal systematic (i.e., predictable, not random) violations of the axioms of EUT [i.e. the standard economic theory of economic behaviour], and the more we look, the more we find. . . . Admitting failure in such cases would be an honourable position . . . but beating the data, or the methods which have generated it, until they become silent, would not.
>
> (Starmer 1999: F8 and F14, see also Rabin and Thaler 2001)

The lack of appreciation of the results of the heuristic and biases approach can at least in part be explained by the same type of arguments previously used to interpret the debate between Keynes and the 'Classics'. Just as Keynes was seen to have adopted the same methodology as Classical economists, so, in the same way, the contributions of the school of Tversky and Kahneman (1983) are explained from the standpoint of the standard methodology of conventional economics. Human behaviour is understood as approximating to a system governed by intrinsic and extrinsic conditions of closure. The vagueness and ever-evolving nature of decision-making is sacrificed in the search for a single and stable law of motion. Heuristics such as representativeness, availability and anchoring and their related biases are considered random and erratic mistakes rather than systematic features of human behaviour. However, Tversky and Kahneman explain that 'the evidence does not seem to support a "truth plus error" model, which assumes a coherent system of beliefs that is perturbed by various sources of distortion and error' (Tversky and Kahneman 1983: 313). In this regard, the heritage of Keynes for modern experimental economists is to acknowledge and defend the particular nature of their analysis. Psychology and experimental economics deal with motives and expectations of agents, and as such the explanations offered can never be presumed to be comprehensive. The non-homogeneity of the material investigated calls for the abandonment of the search for a permanent law of motion. Biases are representative of heuristics that govern perception and judgements, but the organic nature of the decision-making process continually demands new and more appropriate heuristics. Keynes has much to offer modern experimental economists in terms of a methodology that is appreciative of the fuzziness of the disparate and context-dependent ways in which individuals handle decision-making. This methodology recognises the benefits of inferences drawn from general experience, without claiming universality for the results of the research. From this standpoint, experiments and behavioural studies well suit the definition of economics as an engine for the discovery of mechanisms and laws of motion that underlie economic behaviour.

Conclusions

Since Keynes wrote the *General Theory* (1936) many economists have undertaken a critical analysis of the revolutionary aspect of his theory. In 'Mr Keynes and the "Classics"' (1937), Hicks provided a long-lasting interpretation of Keynes's work and its relationship with the 'Classics'. Whatever the current state of health of Keynesian economics, this chapter has argued that the old story of the relationship between Keynes and the 'Classics', which began with Hicks (1937) and continues today with the work of New Keynesian economists such as Akerlof (2002), is a significant story. There is much more to it than the formation of two different economic theories (see, for a similar argument, Young 1987, also Harrod 1937).

Keynes made contributions at both the theoretical and methodological levels, and it is important that these aspects are both considered in any evaluation of the exact nature of his contributions to economics. In particular, this chapter has argued that Keynes proposed to separate explanations based on partial experience from those based on general experience. Similarly, he distinguished between the search for permanent and provisional laws of motion governing economic events. These suggestions are indicative of the distinctiveness of his theory and methodology. Economists referring to the old story of the relationship between Keynes and the 'Classics' would find that these suggestions are useful for the modern development of economics, including the current debate on the role of formalism and experiments in economics.

Part II

From rationality to unemployment and the Monetary Circuit

4 A two-dimensional theory of probability and knowledge

Introduction

The basic proposition of this book is that Keynes's ideas remain a driving force in the development of new theories and methods of economic analysis. In this chapter, this basic proposition is used to explore, and build on, Keynes's analysis of probability and knowledge with the purpose of proposing the foundations for a modern theory of uncertainty.

Uncertainty is a central theme in the economic and philosophical writings of Keynes. It is also a theme of paramount importance in the Keynesian literature, though Keynesian scholars often attach different meanings to it (Chick 1983: 213–217). The *Oxford English Dictionary* defines uncertainty as something not definitely known or knowable. This definition itself is open to different interpretations, e.g. for how long is something not definitely known or knowable? However, and in contrast to standard mainstream economic theory (see, for example, Hammond 1987), this definition allows for the possibility that something may not be knowable. This possibility lies at the heart of Keynes's criticisms of the mainstream economic theory of his time. He argued that the validity of the Classical approach in both probability theory and economic theory was limited to the special case of risk, characterised by the existence of a well-defined probability distribution.

> By 'uncertain knowledge' I do not mean merely to distinguish what is known for certain from what is only probable . . . [in the sense that] the prospect of an European war is uncertain, or the price of copper and the rate of interest twenty years hence. . . . About these matters there is no scientific basis on which to form any calculable probability whatever. We simply do not know.
>
> (Keynes 1937: 113–114)

Keynes thus sought to develop a more general theory of probability, and a fuller appreciation of the nature of uncertainty and its consequences for an economy.

Probability theory and forms of knowledge

Keynes on probability relations

In *A Treatise on Probability* (1921) Keynes is concerned with the analysis of probability relations, i.e. probabilities are conceived as a relation between a conclusion and certain evidence:

$$p = a|h \tag{4.1}$$

where a is the proposition or conclusion, h the set of premises and p the degree of belief that is rational to hold in the proposition a given the evidence h. The probability relation (4.1) has two important features. First, it is a logical relation. Just as no place is intrinsically distant in space, no proposition is intrinsically probable. Probabilities are always relative to certain evidence. Given the set of premises h, the logical conclusion a is fixed in an objective way. In the sense important to formal logic, the probability of any conclusion is thus not subject to human caprice (Keynes 1921: 4).

Second, the probability relation (4.1) is a subjective relation. Probabilities are not a property of the external material reality, but rather a property of the way individuals think about the external material reality. The probability relation (4.1) is thus subjective, because individuals have different reasoning powers and different evidence at their disposal. This means that the acquisition of new evidence, say h_1, does not affect the validity of (4.1), but gives rise to the new probability relation $p_1 = a/h_1 h$ (Keynes 1921: 33). Continuing with the space analogy, when it is said that a place X is, say, five miles away, the implicit assumption is that X is five miles away from a certain starting point. If the starting point is moved, say, two miles closer to X, then, the place will be three miles away. To argue that, as a result of further evidence, p is wrong and that p_1 is correct makes as little sense as to argue that the initial opinion that X was five miles away is wrong, because the place is now only three miles away. Both of the probabilities are correct relative to their evidence. New evidence gives rise to a new probability relation, not a fuller knowledge of the old one (Keynes 1921: 33). In more general terms, it can be argued that probabilities are not an object of knowledge, but simply a form of relational knowledge (Lawson 1988: 42–44). For this reason, Keynes was critical of the realist view of English Empiricists, according to which the probability of an event can be discovered or learned with new evidence (Keynes 1907: 18, see also Carabelli 1985: 155–156, O'Donnell 1989).

In short, Keynes considered his theory of probability to be both (logically) objective and rational (Lawson 1985). For any two individuals faced with the same evidence and reasoning powers, it is rational to hold the same degree of belief in a given proposition. In this sense, the probability of a proposition is objective. Importantly, this objectivity only exists at the level of opinion or knowledge of the external material reality. It is not a property of the external material reality itself (Keynes 1921: 19).

A modern theory of probability and knowledge

In *A Treatise on Probability* Keynes also suggested a plausible link between probability relations and different forms of knowledge. In this regard, he discriminated between the 'primary proposition', *a*, and the secondary proposition or probability relation (4.1). He then went on to distinguish between knowledge of, and knowledge about, the primary proposition *a*, the difference being that the former coincides with *certainty* of rational belief in *a*, whereas the latter corresponds to *probable degrees* of rational belief in the primary proposition *a* (Keynes 1921: 15). Drawing on this distinction, this chapter argues that probability relations can be used to represent a broad variety of degrees of rational belief in the primary proposition or conclusion *a*. In other words, probability relations in Keynes's terms can be used to develop a general theory of knowledge, which includes the case of certain knowledge, probable (or risky) knowledge and uncertain knowledge.

Table 4.1, row 1, shows four possible forms of knowledge that can be derived from different degrees of rational belief. Certainty, which describes the highest degree of rational belief, represents a special case in which the set of premises *h* is known, and also the secondary proposition *p* asserting a certainty relation between the primary proposition *a* and the premises *h* is fully known.[1] In this case, the knowledge of *a* that is implied from *h* is perfect, that is $p = 1$. Thus, certainty represents the upper limit of probable (or risky) knowledge. This interpretation of certain knowledge is also consistent with Keynes's definition of certainty as 'the maximum probability' (see, for instance, Keynes 1921: 16). A less-than-certain knowledge prevails when neither *h* nor the secondary proposition, *p*, are fully known, asserting in this case a probability relation between *a* and *h*. The degree of rational belief in *a* is thus positive, but lower than in the case of certainty. In

---

1 Keynes also discusses the case in which *a* is known directly. See, for this more controversial form of knowledge, Lawson (1987: 957–963).

Table 4.1 Two-dimensional theory of probability and related forms of knowledge

Forms of knowledge	Certainty	Risk	Uncertainty$_1$	Uncertainty$_2$
Degree of rational belief, p	$(p = 1)$	$(0 < p < 1)$	$(0 < p < 1)$	(p non-existent)
Weight of argument, V	High	High	Low	Non-existent

algebraic terms this means that $0 < p < 1$. The form of knowledge that can be derived in this case is traditionally labelled risk.

A more extreme form of knowledge is uncertainty. For the sake of historical accuracy, it should be stressed that Keynes did not explicitly refer to uncertainty in *A Treatise on Probability*. However, this chapter maintains that there are actually two notions of uncertainty which can be derived from the book, namely: (i) uncertainty as probable knowledge based on slight information; and (ii) uncertainty as total absence of probable knowledge, also known as 'pure uncertainty' (see also Lawson 1985: 913–914, Runde 1991: 130–133, Bellofiore 1994: 107–116). In the following discussion, the first type of uncertainty is labelled uncertainty$_1$, and the second type is called uncertainty$_2$.

Keynes's weight of argument and uncertain knowledge type 1 (uncertainty$_1$)

The first notion of uncertainty that can be derived from *A Treatise on Probability* describes situations in which probable knowledge does exist, but it is based on slight information. This is labelled uncertainty$_1$ in Table 4.1. The cause of this form of uncertain knowledge is to be found not in the probability relation p itself, but rather in the very indistinct nature of the set of premises h on which knowledge about a is derived. For this reason, the notion of uncertainty$_1$ comes out in conjunction with the discussion of the concept of weight of argument, V.

$$V = V(a|h) \tag{4.2}$$

In *A Treatise on Probability* Keynes uses three different definitions of weight of argument, namely: (i) the absolute amount of relevant evidence (Keynes 1921: 84); (ii) the balance of the absolute amounts of relevant knowledge and relevant ignorance (Keynes 1921: 77), and (iii) the degree of completeness of information (Keynes 1921: 345). These definitions are not fully consistent, and they are open to different interpretations (Runde

1990: 279–283, Dow 1995c). For instance, an increase in the amount of relevant evidence will increase the weight of argument under definition (i), but this is not necessarily the case under definitions (ii) and (iii). If additional evidence indicates that there is more ignorance than individuals previously believed, the degree of completeness of information will decrease, as will the absolute amount of relevant knowledge compared to relevant ignorance. Since under definitions (ii) and (iii) the weight of argument moves in the same direction, in the rest of the chapter the absolute amount of relevant knowledge (compared to relevant ignorance), and the degree of completeness of information will be used interchangeably.

Keynes's weight of argument V is the second component of the probability theory described in Table 4.1, and, together with the rational degree of belief p, in this chapter is used to define different forms of knowledge. Before doing that, it is important to note that the weight of argument is always affected by new evidence, since it is a measure of the set of premises h on which knowledge about a is derived. For instance, when the amount of relevant evidence h increases, the magnitude of the probability of the argument p may decrease, increase or stay constant, depending upon whether the new knowledge strengthens or weakens the unfavourable or favourable evidence. However, independently from changes in p, the new evidence would always affect the degree of completeness of information on which the primary proposition a is based (Keynes 1921: 80).

Drawing on these ideas, this chapter maintains that Keynes's weight of argument should play an important complementary role to probability relations in a modern theory of practical decision-making (see, for a similar argument, Rottenstreich and Tversky 1997). The probability relation (4.1) represents the degrees of belief p that it is rational to hold in the proposition a given the evidence h. Thus, the probability relation (4.1) states what degree of belief, in preference to alternative degrees of belief, it is rational for individuals to hold on the basis of the evidence h. Moving slightly from theory to practice, this means that the probability relation (4.1) states what degree of belief it is rational for individuals to use as a guide to conduct in preference to alternative degrees of belief. From this perspective, it is therefore rational to be guided in action by probability relations. However, the problem with the use of probability relations in practical decision-making is that in the case of the proposition a being based on slight information h, p is a poor guide to action.[2] In this case, individuals are interested not so much

---

2 The probability relation (4.1) is, of course, completely inadequate in the case of inconclusive premises of the probability relation. See the next section for a discussion of this case.

in the logical relation between a and h, but in the degree of completeness of h, i.e. in the balance between the absolute amounts of relevant knowledge and relevant ignorance on which a is based. Therefore, in situations in which probable knowledge exists but is based on slight information, the weight of argument becomes the decisive factor for convincing individuals that the probability relation is a reliable guide to action.

The weight of argument is represented by a scale of values in Table 4.1, row 2. Depending on the quantity and quality of the evidence h on which the primary proposition a is based, it is possible to discriminate between different degrees of evidential weight. At one end, there is the case of low weight. In this case, the only set of premises h on which the primary proposition a is based is nothing but bare information just sufficient to conceive a probability relation between a and h. Individuals have no other relevant evidence at their disposal, except the information that there is a logical relationship between a and h. This is a case of uncertainty$_1$ in Table 4.1. As the degree of completeness of h increases, the weight of argument rises. But how much will it rise? Drawing on Keynes's work, this chapter maintains that there is not a definite answer to that question, because unlike the case of probability relations, the weight of argument is not gradeable on a cardinal scale (Keynes 1921: 77–80, see also Kregel 1987b: 526, Dequech 1997: 30). This means that it is not possible to speak, say, of $V = 1$ or $0 < V < 1$. It is rather the case of more or less complete information. For this reason, in Table 4.1, row 2, the weight of argument V is measured in terms of high or low. Starting with low V, as new relevant evidence reduces the incompleteness of information, individuals feel less uncertain of their knowledge about a, and hence less uncertain about using probabilities as a guide to action. Ironically, it follows that when the weight of argument is at its maximum level, it becomes irrelevant in practical decision-making. When individuals perceive the set of premises h to be sufficiently complete (i.e. V is high) to imply a rational degree p in the primary proposition a, p becomes prominent and V falls into the background. In other words, the weight of argument loses practical relevance when it is high, and probabilities take centre stage as a guide to action. This is the case of certainty and risk in Table 4.1, row 2.

Uncertainty as absence of probable knowledge: uncertain knowledge type 2 (uncertainty₂ or 'pure uncertainty')

The second notion of uncertain knowledge, uncertainty$_2$, that can be derived from *A Treatise on Probability* results from two cases, namely when probabilities are either (a) unknown or (b) numerically incalculable or incomparable (Keynes 1921: 34–35). Unknown probabilities lead to vague knowledge, at best. That is the case when the probability relation can be calculated, but the reasoning power of individuals is so weak that it prevents relating the premises to the conclusion. Unknown probabilities are a theoretical possibility, but they are not really relevant for the purpose of this chapter. They are simply an acknowledgement of the fact that in some circumstances limited human reasoning does not allow individuals to conceive of a probability relation. For this reason, unknown probabilities, which are the first case of 'pure uncertainty' or uncertainty$_2$, will not be discussed in the rest of this chapter.

By contrast, in the case of numerically incalculable or incomparable probabilities, the uncertain degree of rational belief in the primary proposition a reflects the absolute inconclusive basis of the evidence or premises of the probability relation. If the evidence upon which individuals base their belief is h, then what individuals know, namely the secondary proposition p, is that the primary proposition a bears the probability relation of degree p to the set of premises h; this knowledge justifies individuals to hold a rational belief of degree p in the proposition a. The problem with numerically incalculable or incomparable probabilities is that the evidence h upon which individuals should base their belief is inconclusive, and hence the secondary proposition p cannot be either estimated or used for comparison with other secondary propositions. For this reason, individuals cannot rationally hold any probable degree of belief p in the primary proposition a, i.e. p is simply non-existent. The inconclusiveness of the evidence h also means that the weight of argument V is non-existent. In Table 4.1, uncertainty$_2$ is thus described by p and V being both non-existent. In this case, there is either no information at all, or whatever evidence is available is far below what is required to give meaning to the logical relation between a and h. For this reason, it also makes little sense to speak of different degrees of uncertainty$_2$, as was the case for uncertainty$_1$. Since individuals cannot know probabilities and weight of argument, therefore, uncertainty$_2$ describes the case where individuals show the highest degree of distrust and uneasiness in their practical decision-making. Uncertainty$_2$ is then the most extreme form of uncertain knowledge (see also Carabelli 1988: 42–50).

On the nature of uncertainty

Formal logic versus human logic

The previous sections have discussed two notions of uncertainty that can be derived from Keynes's *A Treatise on Probability*, namely uncertainty$_1$ and uncertainty$_2$. The difference is that in the latter the absolute inconclusiveness of the set of premises h means that a probability relation cannot be conceived, whereas in the former h does exist, and does lead to the formation of probability relations, but given the incompleteness of the set of premises, these probability relations are unreliable as a guide to conduct. Nevertheless, why is there uncertainty$_1$ or uncertainty$_2$ in the first place? In other words, why is the set of premises *h* incomplete to the point that these probability relations become unreliable? Similarly, why is the set of premises *h* inconclusive such that probability relations are non-existent?

In the editorial foreword to the reprint of *A Treatise on Probability*, Braithwaite, a close friend of Keynes at the time he was finishing the book, explains that the main purpose of *A Treatise on Probability* is to argue for probabilities being conceived as a logical relation between a proposition *a* and a set of premises *h* (Braithwaite 1973: xxi). The book does not thus investigate the nature of the quality and quantity of the set of premises *h*. Questions about the degree of completeness of the set of premises *h* or their conclusiveness were not part of the core enquiries of the book. For this reason, these questions were at best only partially answered.

Braithwaite also suggests that Keynes returned to the subject of probability theory with a short review of *Foundations of Mathematics* by Ramsey (Keynes 1931). In the paper Ramsey had criticised Keynes for defending the view that probabilities can be numerically incalculable or incomparable. Keynes rated Ramsey's criticism highly for two reasons (Gerrard 1992b: 86–90, see also Fontana and Gerrard 1999: 313–316). First, it clarified the proper scope of probability relations. The probability calculus represents the set of rules for ensuring consistency within degrees of belief. As such the probability calculus is subject to formal logic, which is concerned with the set of rules of consistent thought. Thus, the proper scope of probability relations is to measure in numerical terms the rationality of the different degrees of belief in a proposition *a* given the evidence *h*. On this point, then, Keynes had to agree with Ramsey that probabilities are always numerically measurable.

Second, Ramsey's criticism pointed the way towards the next area of inquiry in probability theory, namely the evidential basis for the rationality of different degrees of belief (Keynes 1931: 338). Keynes had to concede that *A Treatise on Probability* was mainly a study in formal logic, and for this reason the case for incalculable or incomparable probabilities was not justified. That case could only be granted once the nature of the information used to attach probabilities to primary propositions was fully investigated and explained. To do this, he had to move from formal logic to human logic, and within human logic the focus of the analysis had to be on the possibility of the evidence being inconclusive.

On the nature of the premises of probability relations

In *A Treatise on Probability* Keynes touched on the issue of the evidential basis of the different degrees of belief when discussing the weight of argument. Keynes explained that the weight of argument is of paramount importance in deciding whether or not probability relations are a reliable guide to practical decision-making. Unfortunately, as suggested by Braithwaite, the analysis of weight of argument was secondary to the purpose of the book, and for this reason it was ambiguous and largely incomplete. However, this chapter maintains that in *A Treatise on Probability* Keynes laid the groundwork for his subsequent analysis of the nature of evidential basis of different degrees of belief (see also Winslow 1986: 421–427; Hamouda and Smithin 1988: 160–162). In fact, in the second part of *A Treatise on Probability* Keynes argued that probability relations such as that in equation (4.1) can only be fully justified if it can be assumed that the material on which they are based is made of 'legal atoms', such that each of these atoms exercises its own separate, independent and invariable effect (see, for example, Keynes 1921: 276–278). If this is the case, then complete information of the material reality under investigation can be easily inferred from partial information of its separate components. In other words, given a number of atomistic elements and their connecting laws, it is possible to infer information about the combined effects of these elements, without exhaustive evidence of all possible circumstances. Keynes warned that, unfortunately, this is not always the case. Not all phenomena are atomic, with the result that probability relations like (4.1) are not always justified. Thus, in the final chapters of *A Treatise on Probability* Keynes suggested that the incompleteness or inconclusiveness of the evidential basis of the different degrees of belief is related to the possibility of the non-atomistic nature of the material reality. As argued by Lawson, this is tantamount to an acceptance that probability relations, leading to different forms of knowledge of the external reality, via the weight of argument are associated with a particular view of reality itself (Lawson 2003b: 173–177).

Keynes further clarified his view on the non-atomistic nature of the external reality in a biographical essay on Edgeworth, where he distinguishes natural phenomena from social phenomena, the difference being that whereas the 'atomic hypothesis' works perfectly in the former, it breaks down in the latter (Keynes 1926: 262). The assumption of a uniform and homogeneous continuum of atomistic material is not necessarily satisfied by social phenomena, which are characterised by organic unity, discreteness and discontinuity. In this case, knowledge of the material reality under investigation cannot automatically be inferred, via connecting laws, from knowledge of its separate components. In other words, social phenomena may possess properties which are not derivable from each individual part of them (Rotheim 1988: 83–90). For example, in making an investment decision a producer has to form expectations about the conduct of other producers as well as of consumers. Other producers are naturally compelled to do the same. Therefore, for each producer, what must be known in order to make an investment decision today will be known only when the effects of those decisions take place. In other words, the outcome of a current investment decision cannot be derived from the independent and separate behaviour of each single producer. It is rather the organic interactions of the current conduct of all producers, as well as of consumers, which determine the future outcome of an investment decision (Kregel 1980: 35–38, Carvalho 1988: 74–75). This means that, when constructing probability relations about social phenomena, the set of premises upon which probability relations are based is in some significant way known only *ex post*. The problem then is that if, as in the case of investment decisions, the set of premises is at least partly unknown, hence incomplete or inconclusive, there are no connecting laws on which to draw in order to reduce the paucity of information. Similarly, as further evidence arises, individuals may have problems in connecting it with previous information. More than a decade later, Keynes would refer to this argument when reviewing *A Method and Its Application to Investment Activity* by Tinbergen for the *Economic Journal* (Keynes 1939: 315).

In the late 1930s Tinbergen had carried out some pioneering testing on business cycle theories on behalf of the League of Nations. Keynes was asked to comment on a proof copy of the work. Keynes's main criticism was at the methodological level, namely that Tinbergen had failed to differentiate economics and other social sciences from natural sciences, and that he was mistaken on the nature of the material that is the object of economic investigations. If economic phenomena were the outcome of numerically measurable and independent atomistic factors, then the statistical methods pioneered by Tinbergen could be safely applied to discover the causal mechanisms behind all past, present and future business cycles. However, economic material is not uniform through time, with the result that any generalisation derived from whatever economic statistics are available at a particular point in time must be made with prudence. For this reason, Keynes was sceptical about the general validity of the results obtained by Tinbergen. He later reinforced this point in private correspondence with Harrod.

> I also want to emphasise strongly the point about economics being a moral science. I mentioned before that it deals with introspection and with values. I might have added that it deals with motives, expectations, psychological uncertainties. One has to be constantly on guard against

treating the material as constant and homogeneous. It is as though the
fall of the apple to the ground depended on the apple's motives, on
whether it is worth falling to the ground, and whether the ground wanted
the apple to fall, and on mistaken calculations on the part of the apple
as to how far it was from the centre of the earth.

(Keynes 1938a: 300)

The quote is a lucid exemplification of the argument about the non-atomistic
nature of material reality, which was first put forward by Keynes in the final
chapters of *A Treatise on Probability*. The fall of an apple to the ground
is a natural phenomenon, and as such the atoms that constitute the apple
are regulated, among other things, by the law of gravity. Once this law
is properly understood and formulated, then it can be applied to other
atomistic environments. More generally, once the components of a natural
phenomenon and their connecting laws are discovered, it is possible to use
the knowledge derived from that particular phenomenon in order to explain
other natural phenomena. The case is different for economic phenomena,
where motives, expectations and psychological uncertainties play a prominent role. The possibility of applying generalisations from one phenomenon
to another is limited. In this sense, the non-atomistic features of social reality,
i.e. the lack of 'legal atoms' and 'connecting laws', severely restrict the
degree of conclusiveness and completeness of the information used to build
probability relations about social phenomena.

Paul Davidson and Non-ergodic/Monetary Post Keynesians on uncertainty

Previous chapters of this book have maintained that Keynes had an enor-
mous influence in economics, especially among the group of Post Keynesian
economists. Whatever their many differences, several members of this group
have put a great deal of time and effort into developing Keynes's theory of
probability and knowledge (Lawson and Pesaran 1985, Dow and Hillard
1995, Arestis 1996). This is especially true of Paul Davidson (1972) and
other Non-ergodic/Monetary Post Keynesians such as Kregel (1980) and
Chick (1983: Ch. 17), who have proposed a theory of involuntary unemployment based on the link between uncertainty and money.

The main tenet of Davidson is that there are two paradigms in economics,
namely the economics of a predetermined, immutable and ergodically
knowable reality, and the economics of an unknowable, transmutable and
Non-ergodic reality (e.g. Davidson 1996). The first paradigm is made up of
two groups, depending upon whether full knowledge of reality is obtainable
in any time period (Group 1), or only in the long run (Group 2). Group 1

includes early-twentieth-century Classical models, rational expectations models and new Classical macroeconomic models. Group 2 covers bounded-rationality models and New Keynesian models, as well as standard expected utility models. As for the second paradigm, Davidson refers to the work of Shackle, Old Institutionalist models and modern Post Keynesian monetary models. Since Davidson derives these distinctions with reference to Keynes's writings, it is fruitful to discuss the two economic paradigms in terms of Keynes's general theory of probability and knowledge as summarised in Table 4.1.

The first paradigm describing the economics of a predetermined, immutable and ergodically knowable reality is covered by columns 2 (Certainty) and 3 (Risk) in Table 4.1. Starting with Group 1, Davidson claims that in these models economic reality is assumed to be immutable, and for this reason economic agents have either full knowledge or probable knowledge of the future. The models in Group 2 are slightly different, since they assume that in the short run economic agents have limited knowledge. For this reason, knowledge of the future is incomplete or altogether missing. However, since in its essential features the external reality is fixed, with the passage of time the problem of limited information diminishes, and in the long run economic agents will have either full knowledge or probable knowledge of the future.

Notwithstanding the strength of the distinction made by Davidson between the first and second economic paradigms, the assumption of a predetermined or immutable reality is a sufficient, but not a necessary, condition for achieving certain or probable knowledge. What really counts in terms of Keynes's theory of knowledge is that economic agents have adequate evidence at their disposal, such that it is rational to hold a positive or unitary degree of belief in a proposition about future outcomes. In other words, immutable reality models are a case, possibly the most compelling case, where information is adequate or complete, i.e. V is high, and the probability of argument, p, is equal to one or close to one. However, columns 2 and 3 in Table 4.1 also include transmutable reality type of models describing routine economic decisions. In these cases, again, the degree of belief that is rational for agents to hold is equal to one or close to one, and the evidential basis of these degrees of belief is high.

In the classification by Davidson, the second paradigm in economics champions the view of an unknowable, transmutable and non-ergodic reality. The basic feature of the world in this alternative paradigm is that the future can be profoundly affected by the actions of economic agents, often in ways that are not even remotely foreseeable by these agents. Using an expression familiar to Shackle, in this world 'the choice of agents is genuine, choice matters' (e.g. Shackle 1961: 271–272). In other words, agents are allowed to act in unpredictable ways. For this reason, Davidson argues, in these cases agents do not have, and can never have, any adequate knowledge of the future. They are simply uncertain about the future because, in some profound way, the future is yet to be determined.

The case of uncertain knowledge described by Davidson is represented by column 5 (Uncertainty$_2$) in Table 4.1. In this circumstance, because of the inconclusiveness of the evidential base, probability relations are numerically incalculable or incomparable. Probabilities and weight of argument are said to be non-existent. This pure form of uncertainty is what throughout this chapter has been called uncertainty$_2$. However, this is only one case of uncertain knowledge. In terms of Keynes's theory of knowledge, uncertainty also arises when probability relations do exist, i.e. $0 < p < 1$, but the weight of argument V is low. In Table 4.1, this form of uncertainty is listed in column 4 (Uncertainty$_1$). In this circumstance, it is the incompleteness rather than the inconclusiveness of the evidential base of our knowledge that leads to uncertain knowledge.

As indicated in Table 4.1, uncertainty$_1$ and uncertainty$_2$ are two distinct notions of knowledge, but they are strongly connected to each other by their mutual reference to the evidential base of probability relations (see, for an early view of this idea, Kregel 1987b: 526–528). In both cases uncertainty arises because of what Keynes labelled the non-atomistic feature of economic reality. Economic phenomena are the outcome of individual decisions, which are taken now, and in the times to come, by economic agents. If economic reality were atomistic, it could be assumed that all economic agents were identical in respect of their reasoning powers, current knowledge and past experience. It would then be rational to expect that in similar circumstances agents formulate similar propositions about the future. Economic phenomena will be uniform and homogeneous through time. However, economic reality is not atomistic, and economic phenomena are not uniform and homogeneous through time. In particular, economic agents are not the same, unlike the 'legal atoms' of the falling apple in the previous example. Agents have different experiences and distinct physical make-ups. They therefore make different interpretations of the available evidence and, as a result, they produce different propositions about the future. This means that the evidential base used to assign probability relations is itself 'invented' in the very process of making a decision.

This is as far as the argument about the non-atomistic nature of economic reality goes. In other words, this argument does not mean that economic agents will never be able to form probability relations: sometimes they will, and sometimes they won't. When agents do form probability relations about future events, it means that the degree of completeness of the evidential base is adequate. How adequate is impossible to say in advance, and for this reason in Table 4.1 the weight of argument is represented by a scale of values. When the degree of completeness of information is low, probability relations are formed, but individuals are uncertain about the meaning to attach them in practical decision-making. This is the case of uncertainty$_1$. When agents do not form probability relations about future events, it is because the degree of completeness of the evidential base is inadequate. The weight of argument is non-existent, probability relations are non-existent. This is the notion of uncertainty$_2$. The distinction between the two notions of uncertainty is not only a question of semantics. Uncertainty$_1$ and uncertainty$_2$ differ in their operational implications. They lead to two different though complementary types of economic behaviour, which are explored in the next chapter, which is dedicated to the monetary implications of the Post Keynesian notions of uncertainty.

Conclusions

This chapter has developed a theory of individual knowledge based on a two-dimensional approach to probability theory, namely probability relations and weight of argument. Probability relations provide a rational assessment of the relative degree of belief attached to alternative propositions, whereas the weight of argument measures the evidential base of these degrees of belief. These two components of probability theory allow for a general theory of individual knowledge, which includes the mainstream cases of certainty and risk as well as the non-mainstream case of uncertainty.

5   Uncertainty and money

Introduction

The *Companion to Post Keynesian Economics* (King 2003) contains a wealth of entries on topics broadly related to Post Keynesian economics. However, it has only three entries on books, namely *A Treatise on Probability* (Keynes 1921), *A Treatise on Money* (Keynes 1930) and *The General Theory of Employment, Interest and Money* (Keynes 1936). This may not be too surprising given that Keynes's work and ideas have played a central role in the development of Post Keynesian economics. What is more surprising is that even a cursory reading of these entries shows how unrelated these three books are in the eyes of a great majority of Post Keynesian economists.[1] *A Treatise on Probability* is Keynes's main philosophical work, *A Treatise on Money* is Keynes's most comprehensive and systematic analysis of money and, finally, the *General Theory* is Keynes's revolutionary theory of effective demand and involuntary unemployment.[2] This rigid partition between Keynes's major books is also reflected in three major strands of Post Keynesian economics that have developed out of these books, namely the New Fundamentalist Keynesians, the Monetary Circuit theorists and the Non-ergodic/Monetary Post Keynesians, respectively.

The New Fundamentalist strand of Post Keynesian economics originates with the work of Lawson (1985), and the subsequent books by Carabelli (1988), Fitzgibbons (1988) and O'Donnell (1989). It encompasses the works of those Post Keynesian economists who have recognised the centrality of Keynes's distinct methodology to the understanding of his theories and policies. Therefore, a central theme of the New Fundamentalist research

---

1   For a noteworthy exception, see Chick (1992).

2   This is not to deny that the authors of the three entries in King's book do, in fact, mention some links between the different parts of Keynes's work, but in none of the entries are the three books approached in an homogeneous way.

programme has been the theory of probability and decision-making that Keynes proposed in *A Treatise on Probability* (1921). The Monetary Circuit strand of Post Keynesian economics is mainly related to the works on monetary theory of French and Italian-speaking scholars, such as Parguez (1984) and Graziani (1989). These theorists emphasise the monetary features of modern capitalist economies. They analyse the economic process in terms of the chain of payments, starting with the creation of final means of payment, going on to their successive use in the goods and financial markets and ending with the eventual extinguishment of these final means of payment. For this reason, the main focus of the Monetary Circuit strand of Post Keynesian economics has been the monetary theory developed by Keynes in *A Treatise on Money* (1930). Finally, the Non-ergodic/Monetary strand of Post Keynesian economics has complex origins and features (King 2002), but in this chapter it mainly refers to the theory of uncertainty and unemployment developed by Davidson (1972, 1994) and Kregel (1987b). This theory has featured copiously in many contributions published in the US-based *Journal of Post Keynesian Economics*. Non-ergodic/Monetary Post Keynesians devote a large part of their research to the explanation, and possible solutions, of involuntary unemployment in modern economies. They identify the causes of involuntary unemployment in the working of the principle of effective demand under the (real-world) condition of pure uncertainty, i.e. where there is no scientific basis upon which to calculate a probability relation. Thus, a driving force of the research programme developed by the Non-ergodic/Monetary strand of Post Keynesian economics has been the theory of unemployment offered by Keynes in the *General Theory* (1936).

This chapter is an attempt to show that there is, in fact, an intimate relationship between Keynes's three major books, and hence between these three strands of modern Post Keynesian economics, namely the New Fundamentalist Keynesians, the Monetary Circuit theorists and the Non-ergodic/Monetary Post Keynesians. Building on the two-dimensional theory of probability and connected forms of knowledge presented in the previous parts of this book, the next section relates the second notion of uncertainty (i.e. uncertainty$_2$) to the existence of a long-run demand for a stock of liquid assets and the possibility of involuntary unemployment. Similarly, the final section discusses the intimate though often ignored relationship between the first notion of uncertainty (i.e. uncertainty$_1$) and the existence of a flow of final means of payment and their essential role in the working of modern monetary economies.

Uncertainty, money and involuntary unemployment

Post Keynesian economists are well known for their critical views of recent developments in economics. In particular, they have been on the front line in arguing against the modern New Keynesian search for the microeconomic foundations of macroeconomics (Rotheim 1998). They argue that, if anything, it is microeconomics that is in urgent need of macroeconomic foundations (Crotty 1980, and especially Nasica and Kregel 1999). This paradox is easily explained when the practical implications of the theory of knowledge discussed in Chapter 4 are taken into account.

In Chapter 4 it was argued that there is an intimate link between probability relations, theory of knowledge and individual behaviour. If the probability p is defined as the logical relation between a proposition, a, and a set of premises, h, then when the set of premises is inconclusive, no probability relation can be formed. In this circumstance, it was said that both the weight of argument, V, and the probability, p, are non-existent. It should also be clear by now that the set of premises is often likely to be inconclusive, because of the non-atomistic nature of economic reality. However, if that is the case, then individuals have no knowledge about the proposition a. They may not even be able to form a proposition a, still less a probability about it. In short, individuals are confronted with pure uncertainty. Furthermore, if there is no belief that is rational to hold about the proposition a, then there is nothing to guide individuals in their practical decision-making. There is thus an intimate link between inconclusive evidence, non-existent probability relations and unreliability of probability relations for practical decision-making. This is the notion of uncertainty described by Davidson and other Non-ergodic/Monetary Post Keynesians. But once uncertainty is recognised as a pervasive feature of individual decision-making, what choice is left to economic agents? In answering this question, drawing on Keynes's *General Theory* (1936), some influential scholars of the Non-ergodic/Monetary strand of Post Keynesian economics, such as Davidson (1972: Ch. 2) and Kregel (1980, see also Chick 1983: Ch. 17) have focused their attention on the role of money as a store of wealth. In their view, money is the fundamental macroeconomic institution for coping with the uncertainty of individual decision-making. Liquidity preference (money holding) explains why in modern economies, expenditure may fall short of income, with the result that the sales revenues of producers will not cover all production costs. Losses are then incurred, which in turn lead producers to reduce the level of output and employment. Money is thus, in this perspective, the cause of the failure by the economic system to adjust to the effects of uncertainty (Kregel 1980). In other words, uncertainty$_2$ and money are the building blocks of a modern theory of involuntary unemployment. As indicated in Table 5.1, column 3, this is the first component

Table 5.1 The theoretical implications of uncertain knowledge

	Uncertainty$_1$ (h is incomplete, p is unreliable guide)	Uncertainty$_2$ (h is inconclusive, p is non-existent)
Functions of money	Final means of payment	Store of wealth
Post Keynesian theoretical framework	Modern theory of the Monetary Circuit	Modern theory of involuntary unemployment

of the macroeconomic foundations of the Post Keynesian theory of individual decision-making discussed in Chapter 4.

In modern monetary economies, wages are paid in money, and are either used for buying goods and services or savings. If savings out of wages are positive, then producers have to guess the timing and composition of future demands for goods and services. But if this is the case, wage earners do not know, and cannot know, their future income, because the latter are decided by producers on the basis of their own guesses at the consumption plans of wage earners. In other words, current investment expenditure is related to the expected income of producers, but the latter is based on the expected consumption demand of wage earners, which in turns depends on the investment expenditure of producers. This means that at any moment in time, wage earners and producers lack the knowledge necessary to assure the conditions for equality between current expenditure and current income and, hence, for the achievement of full employment.

As long as savings are used to buy or finance the purchase of investment goods, full employment of all resources, including labour, can still be achieved. In allocating savings between different assets, wage earners are interested in maximising their prospective yields or overall returns. Following Keynes (1936: 222–229), Post Keynesians identify several aspects of the 'yield' of a durable asset, namely the net yield (q), the carrying cost (c), appreciation (a) and the liquidity premium (l) (e.g. Davidson 1994: 54–56). However, for simplicity of discussion, in the rest of this chapter reference is simply made to the 'yield' of a durable asset.

Since in the short run the yield of an asset is inversely related to its price, savers will continue to demand the asset with the highest prospective yield as a store of wealth, until the expansion of its supply causes its yield to fall to equality with the prospective yield of the next-highest-ranked asset. This process continues up to the point at which savings have been allocated to different financial assets, which now give all the same prospective yields. Provided that there is not a bottomless sink of purchasing power, current income is all spent on current output, whether it is consumed or saved to purchase stores of wealth. The reason for the proviso is that money can be a bottomless sink of purchasing power. Money is a special asset, in the crucial sense that its yield is set by the liquidity preference of economic agents, and as such it does not respond, or at least it responds more slowly than other assets, to changes in its supply. This means that when the supply of money expands in response to the increase in the demand for money, its yield, i.e. the short-run interest rate, either does not fall or falls more slowly than the yield on other financial assets. But then, when the interest rate (money yield) is high enough, savers will prefer to hold money to other assets, and money becomes a bottomless sink of purchasing power. The demand to buy or finance investment goods will thus fall short of the value of savings by the amount of money held as a store of wealth. This is to say that current expenditure falls short of current income with the result that the sales revenues of producers will not cover production costs, which then leads producers to reduce the level of output and employment.

There are two important properties of money that should be mentioned at this point. Money has: (i) a zero or very small elasticity of production, and (ii) a zero or small elasticity of substitution with any other asset that has a high elasticity of production (Keynes 1936: Ch. 17). Taking these two properties together, this means that when there is an increase in the demand for money, the level of employment in the production of money or of any other commodity produced by the use of labour services is not affected (Davidson 1972: 222). In terms of the theory of decision-making discussed above, it follows that when uncertainty$_2$ arises, economic agents prefer to hold money rather than buy goods and services or other financial assets. The consequent decline in the demand for labour services in the commodity sector is not then offset by any increase in the demand for labour services in the production of money.

It is thus the liquidity preference of economic agents that makes money a potentially bottomless sink of purchasing power, and its yield high enough to prevent producers from profitably undertaking the full-employment volume of investment. In conclusion, uncertainty$_2$ and the related demand for the stock of money as a store of wealth have a negative effect on the level of effective demand and employment. For this reason, Post Keynesians like Davidson and Kregel insist that once uncertainty is recognised as a pervasive feature of individual decision-making, the macroeconomic result follows that the economic system may settle in equilibrium at a level that falls a long way short of generating full employment (e.g. Kregel 1976: 213–214).[3]

---

3 Theoretically, in these circumstances the economy could settle at any level between zero and full employment.

Uncertainty, money and the production process

It was argued in Chapter 4 that uncertainty$_2$ is only one notion of uncertainty that arises out of the non-atomistic nature of economic reality. When the evidential base does exist but is insufficient to attach a rational degree of belief in a proposition, individual economic agents are again in a condition of uncertainty, and probabilities are an unreliable guide in their practical decision-making. But, as before, once uncertainty is recognised as a pervasive feature of individual decision-making, what choice is left to economic agents? In answering this question, drawing on Keynes's *Treatise on Money* (1930), some influential scholars of the Monetary Circuit strand of Post Keynesian economics have focused their attention on the role of money as a final means of payment (see, for a review of recent contributions, Fontana and Realfonzo 2005). In this role, money defines the context in which modern economic activities are carried out. Money as a final means of payment is the essential macroeconomic institution for coping with the uncertainty of individual decision-making in production activities. In other words, uncertainty$_1$ and money are the building blocks of a modern theory of the Monetary Circuit. As is indicated in Table 5.1, column 2, this is the second, though often ignored, component of the macroeconomic foundations of the Post Keynesian theory of individual decision-making discussed in Chapter 4.

Among the contributions of the Monetary Circuit strand of Post Keynesian economics, the work of Augusto Graziani is prominent (e.g. Graziani 1989, 2003). The basic starting point of Graziani is that there is a substantial continuity in Keynes's writings, but he maintains that the most accurate description of the working of a monetary economy is to be found in *A Treatise on Money* (1930), as well as in the 1937–39 post-*General-Theory* essays, rather than in the 1936 masterpiece (Graziani 1991). In this regard, it is convenient to start the analysis of Graziani's work by reference to the surviving early drafts of Keynes's *General Theory*, where Keynes sets out his fundamental differences with Classical theory in terms of the distinction between a C-M-C′ economy and an M-C-M′ economy (Keynes 1979: 81). The C-M-C′ economy is a neutral money economy, in which production is organised on the basis of the real returns to the factors of labour and capital. Production is thus undertaken up to the point at which the agreed shares of the final output to labour and capital are just sufficient to compensate for the marginal disutility of supplying further labour and capital services. In this sense, the C-M-C′ economy is a co-operative economy. Individual self-interest and maximisation of social welfare are fully consistent. In this economy, the only role of money, if any, is to facilitate the exchange of goods and services. Money is only used 'for purposes of transitory convenience' (Keynes 1979: 81). By contrast, the M-C-M′ economy is an entrepreneur economy in which individual behaviour is motivated by monetary objectives. The purchases of labour and capital services, as well as the exchange of goods and services, are the means of achieving monetary returns. Thus, in the M-C-M' economy, production is undertaken to achieve monetary not real returns. In a very fundamental sense, money defines the context for economic behaviour. For this reason, Graziani argues that in order to understand the working of a monetary economy, and how it differs from a barter economy, it is essential to explain how the flow of means of payment is created, how it circulates and how it is transformed into a stock of money balances (Graziani 1989, 2003: Ch. 3, see also Smithin 1994: Ch. 1, Parguez 1996). In short, the description of a monetary economy calls for an analysis of the monetary circuit.

The simplest model of the theory of Monetary Circuit usually considers a closed economy with no state sector. It can be described by a five-stage triangular relationship between the following groups of agents: the banking system, producers or firms, and wage earners (Realfonzo 1998: Ch. 1, Fontana 2000: 33–37, Graziani 2003: 26–31). The triangular relationship is at the heart of the theory of Monetary Circuit, which considers money as an indirect debit–credit relation between producers and wage earners, inter-mediated by the banking system. This triangular relationship is represented in Figure 5.1.

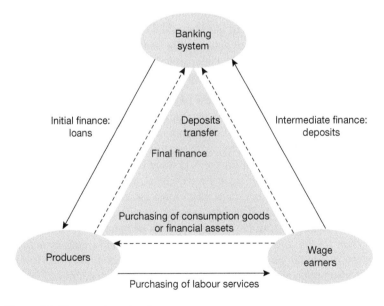

Figure 5.1 The monetary circuit

The base of the triangle represents the contracting between producers and wage earners in the labour market and commodities (goods and financial) markets, respectively. By contrast the left- and right-hand sides of the triangle show the essential role of the banking system in the economic process as the intermediate player of the financial transactions between these two groups of agents.

Stage One: Starting with the analysis of the labour market, on the basis of their expected level of demand for commodities, producers negotiate the wage rate and the level of employment, i.e. the wage bill, with wage earners. If producers are considered as a whole, then other current production costs, including purchases of machinery, and rent can be neglected because they are internal to the sector itself, and the wage bill represents the only expense producers have. This also means that the wage bill represents the credit requirement that producers negotiate with the banking system. Once the negotiations about the amount of credit and the level of interest rate are concluded, the banking system grants creditworthy producers the requested loans, the so-called initial finance.

Stage Two: The initial finance is then immediately used by producers to buy labour services from wage earners. Therefore, at the end of all transactions on the labour market, producers are indebted to the banking system for the same amount that wage earners are credited by it. In Figure 5.1, the plain line shows the transformation of the original loans, i.e. initial finance created by the banking system at the request of producers, into the so-called intermediate finance, namely deposits held at the banking system by wage earners.

Stage Three: The production process takes place. Importantly, the theory of the Monetary Circuit assumes that the decisions concerning the employment level, the amount of consumption and the investment goods to be produced rest completely with producers. Looking at the base of the triangle represented in Figure 5.1, wage earners bargain for nominal wages with producers, since the price level, and therefore the real wage, is only known at a later stage, when wage earners use their bank deposits to buy the newly produced consumption goods. If producers only offer the exact amount of consumption goods demanded by wage earners, then the price expectations of the latter are confirmed, as are their expected real wages. In any other case, changes in the price level of consumption goods will reconcile, via the mechanism of forced savings, the expenditure plans of wage earners with the autonomous decisions of producers.

Stage Four: Wage earners use their bank deposits to buy consumption goods and financial assets in the goods and financial markets, respectively. In accordance with previous assumptions, investment goods are not bought by wage earners, at least not directly, but they are exchanged between producers. Of course, wage earners can buy investment goods indirectly, through the purchase of financial assets offered by producers. In Figure 5.1, the dotted line shows the transfer of bank deposits from the accounts of wage earners to the accounts of producers, via transactions in the two markets. This is the so-called final finance, because it is a measure of the total returns to producers from the sale of consumption goods and financial assets. To the extent that wage earners do not use all their bank deposits in these markets, i.e. as long as wage earners use some intermediate finance to increase their own cash balances, final finance is lower than initial finance, and hence producers are unable to pay back all the original bank loans. The increased cash balances are a net addition to the stock of bank deposits in circulation. They are also a measure of both the debt of producers and the credit of wage earners with the banking system.

Stage Five: At this point, if all deposits are spent, producers can repay their initial bank loans. The monetary circuit is closed. Wage earners obtain the portion of the total production that they have bought in the consumption goods market. Producers get the portion of the total production that they plan to use in their own future production processes (Graziani 2003: Ch. 5).[4] At the end of the circuit, it is thus confirmed that, in the theory of Monetary Circuit, wage earners are limited in their expenditure plans by the wage bill, whereas producers have unlimited spending power, at least as long as the banking system grants them credit.

An important implication of the above analysis, though a step never explicitly made by Graziani and other contributors to the Monetary Circuit strand of Post Keynesian economics (see for example Parguez and Seccareccia 2000), is that the distinction between a barter economy and a monetary economy really falls back on the pervasiveness of the notion of uncertainty$_1$ described in Chapter 4 (see also Fontana 2000).[5] In other words,

---

4 If it is assumed that producers set the price of consumption goods as a mark-up over production costs, then the mark-up is also a measure of the total profits of producers.

5 The possibility of natural disasters does create uncertainty, but this type of uncertainty is exogenous to the economic system and for this reason is not a discriminatory feature of the two types of economies. What distinguishes an entrepreneur economy from a neutral

whereas the analysis of the monetary circuit is an essential element in the study of the nature and origin of money in modern economies, it needs to be complemented by a study of decision-making under conditions of uncertainty.

The analysis of the monetary circuit explains the role of a final means of payment in the production process, but why is there a demand for a flow of a final means of payment in the first place? In other words, why does a monetary circuit occur? The answer lies in the presence of uncertainty$_1$ which, as it was argued in Chapter 4, pervades the employment of labour services (and capital services), as well as the exchange of goods and services. It is the existence of uncertainty$_1$ during the production process described above that calls for a final means of payment to cope with it. In a world of certainty (Table 4.1, column 2), there is no need for a final means of payment. A wage earner could offer labour services to a producer at time t, confident in the knowledge that the claim to goods and services in return for these services will be met by a transfer of a producer or trader at time $t+n$, while a producer may extinguish the initial bank debt by selling goods and services at some other time to some other wage earner or trader. In other words, in a world of certainty all activities between a wage earner and a producer or trader are fixed at the very outset of the economic system. However, if there is uncertainty$_1$, the producer may be unable to sell goods and services, and the wage earner could not then be confident that the claim on goods and services will necessarily be met at some future date (Shackle 1971, Goodhart 1989a: 25–29). It is this possibility of defaulting on obligations that calls for a final means of payment to meet and alleviate the problem of exchanging under conditions of uncertainty$_1$.

It is worth clarifying that even in a world of risk, there is no need for a final means of payment. As discussed in Chapter 4, risk describes a less-than-perfect knowledge, when neither the set of premises h nor the secondary proposition p, asserting a probability relation between the primary proposition a and the premises h, are fully known. In this case, the degree of rational belief in a is positive, i.e. $0 < p < 1$, but lower than the case of certainty. Risk is thus a certainty-equivalent form of knowledge. As in the case of certainty, in a world of risk the whole time path of the economy can be determined at the outset of the economic system, before production, accumulation and exchange activities proceed along prearranged lines. However, whereas in the case of certainty, the outcome of the economic

money economy is the unpredictability of the complex interdependencies of individual choices. This non-atomistic feature of economic reality, which was discussed in Chapter 4, characterises an entrepreneur, but not a money neutral or, for that matter, barter economy.

system is fully known, i.e. all economic activities proceed along one, single, perfectly known prearranged path, in the case of risk economic activities proceed according to one of the probable paths, out of the finite set of possible outcomes of the economic system. In other words, in the case of risk a wage earner, a producer or trader has to prepare for a finite set of probable outcomes by exchanging claims on contingent commodities, e.g. a claim for commodity *x* to commodity *y* if outcome *z* would occur. This also means that in a world of risk money may be used, though, to use Keynes's words, 'merely as a neutral link between transactions in real things and real assets . . . [money] does not enter into motives or decisions' (Keynes 1933a: 408). In short, the monetary circuit that characterises modern economies, together with the nature of money as an indirect credit–debit relationship, can only be understood in a world of decision-making under conditions of uncertainty.

Conclusions

This chapter has argued that the general theory of individual knowledge discussed in previous parts of the book is strictly related to the theories of money developed by two major strands of Post Keynesian economists, namely the Monetary Circuit theorists and the Non-ergodic/Monetary Post Keynesians, respectively. There is indeed an intimate link between what in Chapter 4 have been labelled uncertainty$_1$ and uncertainty$_2$, on the one hand, and the roles of money as a final means of payment and a store of wealth, on the other. The difference between uncertainty$_1$ and uncertainty$_2$ is that in the latter the absolute inconclusiveness of the evidential base of the degrees of belief means that a probability relation cannot be conceived. By contrast, in the former some evidential base exists, and it leads to the formation of probability relations, but, given the incompleteness of this evidence, these probability relations are an unreliable guide to decision-making. This distinction is important when explaining the competing claims of the Monetary Circuit, and the Non-ergodic/Monetary strands of Post Keynesian economics. When Post Keynesians like Paul Davidson argue that uncertainty is the cause of involuntary unemployment, they are actually referring to the causal role of uncertainty$_2$ in order to explain the demand for money as store of wealth, together with the related possibility of prolonged depressions and mass unemployment. Similarly, when Monetary Circuit theorists like Graziani refer to the natural association between the origin and development of the production process, on the one hand, and the creation, circulation and destruction of flows of a final means of payment, on the other, they are actually referring to the causal role of uncertainty$_1$ in order to explain the monetary context of the production process. Finally, taking together the theory of individual knowledge and the theories of money discussed above, this chapter supports the Post Keynesian claim that the obsessive search in modern economics for the microeconomic foundations of macroeconomics is fallacious because, if anything, it is microeconomics that is in urgent need of macroeconomic foundations. The microeconomic foundations of macroeconomics must thus be complemented by the macroeconomic foundations of microeconomics (Harcourt 2006: 3). Money in its dual role of final means of payment and store of wealth is the fundamental macroeconomic institution for coping with uncertainty in its dual form of uncertainty$_1$ and uncertainty$_2$, which characterise microeconomic decision-making.

Part III
Understanding endogenous money

6 Hicks as an early precursor of endogenous money theory

Introduction

On the occasion of the first annual Hicks Lecture, Solow informed the audience that for many young scholars Hicks is merely a great name, a past master of the economics discipline (Solow 1984: 13). Hicks is the author of 'A suggestion for simplifying the theory of money' (1935), *Value and Capital* (1939) and, between these works, 'Mr Keynes and the "Classics"' (1937) that led to the creation of the typical Keynesian *IS-LM* model, mentioned in Chapter 3. Solow called this young Hicks 'J.R.'. However, he said, there is also another Hicks, Sir John (see, on that distinction, Hicks himself, 1975: 36, Harcourt 1975: 368 and also Collard 1993: 332). This mature Hicks is the author of a rather long list of critical writings on contemporary economics, to which J.R. himself had greatly contributed. To mention but a few books, Sir John was the author of *Critical Essays in Monetary Theory* (1967), *The Crisis in Keynesian Economics* (1974), *Causality in Economics* (1979) and *A Market Theory of Money* (1989). The plea of Solow to young scholars is that Hicks's writings have continual relevance. In particular, Solow argues that modern generations of economists can learn important lessons not only from the early Hicks, i.e. J.R.'s writings, but also from the later and more critical Hicks, i.e. Sir John's writings. This chapter responds to Solow's plea by showing that some of the writings of J.R. and Sir John can be used to shed light on key issues discussed in the previous chapters, and in this way they give further strength to the main proposition of this book, namely that Keynesian economics, broadly defined as the economic approach that finds inspiration in Keynes's work, remains a driving force in the development of new theories and methods of analysis (see, on this point, Hicks himself, 1980).

Hicks was greatly influenced by the work of Keynes and, in his own personal and original way, confronted many Keynesian themes, including the role of uncertainty, money and time in modern economic theories and methods. In particular, this chapter explores some of Hicks's writings on money and time. In the Hicks Lecture mentioned above, Solow discusses several criticisms made of Hicks's *IS-LM* model. He defends J.R.'s construction for its use of the fix-wage assumption, the theory of expectations and the particular treatment of stock-flow and information failure problems. He explains the open-ended problematic nature of these assumptions, before discussing the role of the *IS-LM* model in modern economics. However, there is another issue in 'Mr Keynes and the "Classics"', to which Solow refers only briefly, that was an important, though generally neglected, concern of Sir John: the endogeneity of the money supply.[1]

> we can now generalize our *LL* curve a little. Instead of assuming, as before, that the supply of money is given, we can assume that there is a given monetary system – that up to a point, but only up to a point, monetary authorities will prefer to create new money rather than allow interest rates to rise.
>
> (Hicks 1937: 140)[2]

> The model that has just been described should have its uses in the teaching of post-Keynesian (and 'post-Radcliffe') monetary theory; but the temptation to develop it in that direction is one that I must here resist.
>
> (Hicks 1965: 287)[3]

1   The suggestion that the early Hicks has advanced important propositions for the analysis of the endogeneity of the money supply is also supported by Leijonhufvud (1984: 42), and especially Laidler (1999: 317).

2   The quote is part of the last section of the paper in which Hicks shows how the *IS-LM* apparatus could be used to move beyond Keynes's theory towards what he calls 'The Generalized General Theory' (Hicks 1937: 139). His argument is that over a range, the central bank holds the discount rate constant and acts as lender of last resort, but if the increase in high-powered money is deemed 'excessive' the central bank raises the discount rate. The above quote continues as follows: 'Such a generalized *LL* curve will then slope upwards only gradually – the elasticity of the curve depending on the elasticity of the monetary system (in the ordinary monetary sense)' (Hicks 1937: 140).

3   In the rest of the chapter entitled 'Keynes after growth theory' Hicks goes on to explain the theoretical context of his resistance. A credit money model *à la* Wicksell is used to explain the influence of liquidity preference on the whole structure of yields and interest rates. This was his own way, a very sketchy way as he admitted (Hicks 1965: 284), of showing the modern relevance of money-holding on the equilibrium level of income and unemployment (Keynes's 'vision of the day of judgement' in the words of Pigou). More importantly the declared purpose of that chapter was to introduce money into the study of growth equilibrium and of optimal growth paths. Of course, as he explained, there was not much more that he could have said on money within that context (Hicks 1965: 291).

When the bank makes a loan it hands over money, getting a statement of debt . . . in return. The money might be taken from cash which the bank had been holding, and in the early days of banking that may often have happened. But it could be all the same to the borrower if what he received was a withdrawable deposit in the bank itself. The bank deposit is money from his point of view, . . . but from the point of view of the bank, it has acquired the security, without giving up any cash; the counterpart, in its balance-sheet, is an increase in its liabilities. There is expansion, from its point of view, on each side of its balance-sheet. But from the point of view of the rest of the economy, the bank has 'created' money. This is not to be denied.

(Hicks 1989: 58)

Another important, though often ignored link between the early writings of Hicks and his later, more critical, work is the particular nature of methods in monetary theory. Quite early on, J.R. realised that in a Walrasian system of interconnected markets there is no analytical role for money (Hicks 1933: 33–35, see also Hicks 1973: 137–139). Money is the *numéraire* of the economy and, more importantly, it is the medium of exchange used to meet future payments. Thus, in mature monetary economies, money has two main features: (i) money has no intrinsic value; and (ii) it is universally accepted for trading goods and services. If money does not have a value *per se*, and yet agents hold it, Hicks argues, this is simply due to the need to have a means of meeting future payments. But, if the dates and the amounts of future payments are certain, i.e. if agents live in the world of certainty described by a simultaneous general equilibrium model (see Table 4.1 above), how is it possible to have a demand for money as a final means of payment? As matters stood in the 1930s, this was a very difficult question (Hahn 1973b: 162). One way of avoiding the question was to argue that money was another financial asset, and as such it was part of a general theory of portfolio choice. Its role as a store of value in a world of risk then became the distinguishing feature of money,[4] whereas its functions as a means of payment and unit of account were neglected (Laidler 1990: 483, also Pekkarinen 1986: 337–343). But the question still stood (Hicks 1991: 372).

In short, the analysis of the supply of money and the particular nature of methods to be used in monetary theory were two of the important issues that J.R. left for Sir John to discuss. These issues are related to key propositions about the organic nature of the economic reality and the vagueness of human

---

4 For a general discussion of the role of money in a world of certainty and risk, see Chapter 5 above.

knowledge, discussed in previous chapters. More importantly, they are of particular interest to the modern theory of endogenous money, which will be examined in the remaining part of the book. For this reason, Hicks's writings on money and time are the main concerns of this chapter.

'Monetary theory is in "history"': an analytical and historical question

Since the publication of 'A suggestion for simplifying the theory of money' (1935), Hicks has played a leading role in the development of modern economics. Hagemann and Hamouda (1994) have argued that the name of Hicks is synonymous with economics, and Shackle (1991) put him in the Olympus of great economists, together with Marshall and Keynes (see also Hahn 1994: 26). Hicks wrote at length on money covering a period of more than six decades (Leijonhufvud 1981, 1984). He also discussed methods in economics; the two topics were not independent in his mind. He considered monetary issues of special interest for economists. These issues could hardly be explained unless they were looked at historically. The aphorism that Hicks was never tired of using is that monetary theory is in history (e.g. Hicks 1982: xii).

A serious risk in interpreting this aphorism is to take it at face value, without a critical understanding of the methodological issues raised by monetary theory. On first reading, the message of the aphorism is that the nature of money varies dramatically between societies and over time, and hence monetary theory cannot be ahistorical. Hicks is not immune from criticism, because although he most of the time insisted that monetary theory is influenced by contemporary events (e.g. Hicks 1937: 156), that is only one way of looking at monetary issues. In his monetary writings as well as his methodological and more critical writings (e.g. Hicks 1967b, 1974, 1979, 1985, 1989), Hicks suggests that the nature and roles of money can be properly studied only in terms of an economy moving through time. For this reason, monetary issues need to be discussed with the help of dynamic methods of analysis. Thus, the notion that monetary theory is historically conditioned should be interpreted in two rather different ways.

On the one hand, according to Hicks, monetary theory is intrinsically related to real events such that it is impossible to deal with money properly without serious scrutiny of actual events. Monetary theory mainly unfolds under the pressure of current facts. Hicks records the great progress in monetary theory made by Keynes and, before him, by Ricardo. For instance, he explains that in *A Treatise on Money* (1930) Keynes dealt with the dramatic problems due to the restored gold standard. In a similar way, Ricardo wrote about money because of the inflation due to the British war against Napoleon. From this perspective, advances in monetary theory are often the outcome of challenges from real-world problems.

On the other hand, in what now appears to be a more controversial and less popular understanding, Hicks suggested that an appropriate dynamic analysis must be used if monetary issues are to be confronted rather than contained by the old artifices of static analysis. As he said, 'steady state economics . . . has encouraged economists to waste their time upon constructions that are often of great intellectual complexity but which are so much out of time, and out of history, as to be practically futile and indeed misleading' (Hicks 1976: 291).

If it is accepted that there were two ways in which monetary theory was historically conditioned, for Hicks it was increasingly evident that these two understandings were closely linked. He became more and more critical of the way in which, in his early writings, he had separated monetary history from dynamic methods of analysis. He highlighted the radical changes in the structure of modern monetary systems, and insisted that these transformations called for new analytical methods of analysis (Hicks 1967a: 158). In other words, the standard tool of static theory had limited power for the analysis of monetary issues.

In his search for dynamic methods of analysis and their applications to monetary theory,[5] Hicks was aided by the knowledge of the work of the Stockholm school (e.g. Hicks 1976: 283). In particular, Hicks was aware that the limitations of steady state analysis caused Lindahl to abandon his initial attempt to explain changes in the price level (Lindahl 1929), and forced him to develop a genuine dynamic theory in which expectations played a crucial role.

In this regard, it is worth noting that Hansson has discovered a draft paper by Lindahl that formed the core of the essay 'The dynamic approach to economic theory' (Lindahl 1939). This draft was written during the autumn of 1934, and the very beginning of 1935 (Hansson 1982: 196). Thus, when Hicks first encountered Lindahl in the summer of 1934, and again in 1935 (Hicks 1973: 143), the latter had already worked out the sequence analysis as well as his general vision of dynamic theory. It is also important to note that in January 1934 Lindahl visited Cambridge and met Keynes (Lindahl 1934a). At the end of that year, he sent Keynes a draft of a short paper entitled 'A note on the dynamic pricing problem', where he explained the role of expectations (and imperfect foresight) in a single period of time, and

---

5 For a reconstruction of the methodological aspects of Hicks's work, see Leijonhufvud (1984: 28), Collard (1984: 5), Mahloudji (1985: 287–288), Samuels (1993: 359–363) and Currie and Steedman (1990: 108).

in the sequences of these periods (Lindahl 1934b: 131). It is therefore not unnatural to speculate that in the early thirties there were very interesting discussions between Hicks, Keynes and Lindahl (and members of the Stockholm school, more generally) about analytical methods, particularly how they went on to develop the dynamic analysis of their theoretical work, especially in monetary economics. In any case, it is clear that in the search for a dynamic approach to monetary theory, Hicks attached increasing importance to expectations, for the emphasis on expectations necessarily introduces time into economic theory in a non-trivial way. This led to the original distinction between the analysis of a single period and continuation analysis.

Single period theory vs. continuation theory

In his late methodological and more critical writings, Hicks maintained that the aim of dynamic analysis is to describe the working of real economic systems. For this reason, he proposes sequential over contemporaneous causal analyses (Hicks 1979: Chs 5–7). In other words, he recommends focusing attention on the causal chain of historical events that characterise modern economic systems.

The first suggestion in building a proper dynamic analysis concerns the role played by the interval of time, i.e. the lags, through which an economic activity develops from a preceding one (Hicks 1985: 70). Hicks suggests considering the process of economic change being made by a sequence of stages, or what he called single or accounting periods. The analysis of a single period is an essential first step towards the full description of the process. It serves to simplify the handling of the complexities of a changing economy. Besides, as he explains, when agents make decisions, they intend them to be implemented in a stage-by-stage temporal frame. It is thus not only for theoretical convenience, but also for the realism of the study that, at the initial stage of the research, a single period analysis has to be considered superior to continuous analysis. Then, in order to keep the time sequence right, single periods need to be fitted together to provide what Hicks calls a continuation theory, which is concerned with the effects of the events of a single period upon expectations and plans that themselves determine the events of successive single periods (Hicks 1956: 223).[6]

---

6   Hicks had already used period analysis in *Value and Capital* (1939), but he soon became dissatisfied with the temporal device used in that book. He later explained that there were problems *within* the week (as he then called the single period) and *between* weeks. 'Much too much had to happen on that "Monday"! And, even if that was overlooked (as it should

The dynamic analysis put forward by Hicks is therefore a particular sequential theory. The study of the process of economic change is split into the study of what happens *within* a single period (or accounting period) and the study of linkages *between* single periods. In the former, what is under investigation is the process of economic change on the assumption of unchanging expectations. By contrast, in the case of an analysis of linkages between periods, the so-called continuation theory, the analysis allows for the effects on the economic process of changing expectations. From this perspective, the single period becomes the minimum effective unit of time for dynamic economic analyses.

It is of interest to note that a similar notion of time period can also be found in Keynes's analysis of expectations. Soon after the publication of *A Treatise on Money* (1930), Keynes became dissatisfied with his book (Fontana 2003a), and he started to work regularly on what would become the *General Theory* (1936). In a typed fragment of a chapter titled 'Definitions and ideas relating to capital: the concept of accounting period' written in 1933, one of the famous Tilton (Keynes's country house) laundry-basket papers (Keynes 1933c), he talked at length about the distinction between the accounting period and the production period. Keynes referred mainly to the behaviour of entrepreneurs. He held that it was of great convenience for analysts to distinguish two sub-periods within the overall period of production. He argued that normally entrepreneurs have two sets of decisions to make which correspond to different states of expectations. They have to decide how much money to spend in purchasing capital equipment, and how much labour to employ with this capital. The former type of decision defines the production period, whereas the latter determines the accounting period. He then explained that the main feature of the accounting period lies in the fact that all decisions regarding the employment of workers depend exclusively on expectations covering this period (Keynes 1933c: 74).

The typed fragment did not survive in the final version of the *General Theory*, but the notion of accounting period was used for linking short-term entrepreneurial expectations to employment. According to Keynes, whatever happens within the accounting period, entrepreneurs cannot change their employment decisions. In fact, if they do, then by doing it, they will activate a new accounting period (Keynes 1936: 47, note 1). In other words, within the accounting period entrepreneurs hold constant expectations. For his part, Hicks seems to have adopted a similar notion of unit of economic time (see

not have been overlooked) I was really at a loss how to deal with the further problem of how to string my "weeks" and my "Mondays" together' (Hicks 1976: 290, 1985: 69–70, see also Clower and Leijonhufvud 1975, Leijonhufvud 1984: 31–32).

also Lindahl 1934b: 124), though he extended the notion of accounting period beyond the case of entrepreneurial action (Hicks 1985: 94).

Going back to the relationship between single period and continuation analyses, the end of a single period is what Hicks calls the equilibrium at a point of time. This equilibrium represents a point of rest for the economy, in the sense that agents have reached their preferred position (Hicks 1985: 20, see, for a different interpretation, De Vroey 1999: 40). However, and this is the peculiar feature of a dynamic analysis, for Hicks a single period analysis is always the first step in a dynamic theory. It is in the nature of an economic theory over time that activities within each single period give rise to effects over more than that single period of time, with the result that a continuation theory must follow a single-period theory. Dynamic analysis must unveil what happens over the chain of single periods.

Hicks is also explicit about the nature of the link between single periods. He argues that a comparison of what happens in a single period with what was expected to happen is the crucial passage towards continuation theory. Some of these differences could be due to exogenous factors, but the more interesting ones are those traceable to inconsistencies between the plans of the various agents (Hicks 1956: 223). Continuation theory is then the crucial tool to open each single period to the influence of past and future expectations of economic agents. The focus of the theory is then on the rules of conduct that make the transition process from *ex post* results of a single period to the *ex ante* decisions of the next one. These rules determine the conditions that explain the passage from one period to another.

The distinction between single period analysis and continuation analysis is highly original, though little known and used in modern economics. In the remaining part of this chapter, these two different dynamic methods of analysis are briefly related to the critical realism methodology, discussed in Chapter 2, and then used to introduce the modern contributions of endogenous money theory, which are examined in the Chapters 7 and 8. The main objective is to show that the most prominent and often controversial features of the endogenous money theory, namely the debit–credit nature of modern money, the role of the banking system in the production and accumulation process and the origin of recent financial innovations, can be rendered intelligible by Hicks's methods of analysis.

Time and method in endogenous money theory

Over the last two decades there has been a plethora of writings on endogenous money. Against the Neoclassical view that capitalist economies are a sort of multi-barter economy in which all transactions happen simultaneously and that the money supply changes at the whim of the central bank, and only affects variables in the monetary sector via the Classical quantity theory of money, endogenous money theorists argue that money with its debit–credit nature is an essential feature of modern economies[7] and is certainly not a 'veil' (Arestis 1992: 201). Money enters into the economic system through the private initiatives of its main agents, especially firms and consumers of durable goods, and it modifies the inner workings of both real and monetary sectors of the economy. Chapters 7 and 8 analyse the theoretical issues of the endogenous money literature, with the purpose of discussing similarities and differences between its two major approaches, namely the Horizontalist (or accommodationist) approach and the Structuralist approach. In the remainder of this chapter, the focus of the discussion is on the methodological features of endogenous money theory. The reason for this, as will be become clearer later in the book, is that some of Hicks's ideas on money and time can profitably be used to resolve some controversial issues between the Horizontalist and Structuralist approaches to endogenous money.

Money plays various roles in modern economies. This is one of the most important lessons to be learned from the early writings by Hicks, as well as from his later and more critical writings. Money as a flow of final means of payment is tied into the production decisions of firms and the expenditure decisions of consumers, whereas as a store of wealth it is held in the portfolios of savers.[8] How then is it possible to reconcile these functions? These roles should both be given importance in a sound monetary theory but, as Hicks has suggested, this means abandoning steady-state analysis for dynamic methods of analysis. Following Hicks's ideas, this section argues that it is possible to discriminate between a single period analysis of the money supply process, in which basic functional relationships are laid out, and a continuation analysis of the money supply process, through which more complex issues can be addressed. It is worth noting that the distinction between a single period analysis and a continuation analysis of the money supply process is consistent with the methodology of diversity which, as discussed in Chapter 2, is a core characteristic of modern Post Keynesian economics. It is also in harmony with the emphasis in critical realism on open system theorising. It provides simple and realistic causal explanations for economic events, whilst recognising the complexity of the social and institutional context of human behaviour. Furthermore, it is naturally based

---

7 See, on the indirect debit–credit of modern money, the discussion of the work of Graziani (e.g. 1989) in Chapter 5.

8 The Monetary Circuit strand of Post Keynesian economics holds a similar view. See Chapter 5 above, especially Figure 5.1.

on a non-atomistic vision of economic reality, which was discussed in Chapters 4 and 5.

A single-period theory of money starts from the proposition, discussed in Chapter 2, that reality is made of a complex interaction of facts and events (actual reality), experience and impression (empirical reality), and structures and mechanisms that order events (non-actual reality). It also holds that the focus should not be on facts and their relations, but rather on the mechanisms and tendencies that regulate these facts. A single-period theory of money thus aims at simple and stable relationships that may be obscured, or at best difficult to disentangle, once all the complexities of the modern monetary economies are considered. A single period model is based on the simplifying assumption that within the period considered agents hold constant expectations. This assumption helps to interpret real causal structures as temporally stable, though not inherently predictable, and in this way it helps to detect the mechanisms and tendencies regulating actual events. In practice, a single-period theory of money will continue for a sufficiently long period of time for the effects of the process of circulation of money triggered by the production decisions of firms, to become apparent, or, what is the same thing, for the effects on income and employment of the circulation of money to be revealed.

The drawback of a single-period theory of money is that this type of analysis traces out the effects of a demand-driven increase in the quantity of money on the assumption that the expectations of agents, as reflected in their liquidity preferences, do not change within that period. However, one of the effects of a monetary expansion is to influence the liquidity preference of all economic agents involved (Hicks 1976: 288). In other words, the simplifying assumption of holding the expectations of agents constant allows the detection of mechanisms and tendencies regulating the actual effects of a demand-driven increase in the quantity of money. However, one of the possible consequences of the latter is to make the newly discovered real causal structures unstable.

There are thus evident limits to the analytical questions that can be answered within the time frame of a single period analysis. A single-period theory of money should be used as a simple device to separate out the effects of constant expectations from the effects of disappointments and changes in the state of expectations. In other words, looking at the period by itself, it is appropriate and very convenient to assume that the economy is initially in a state of rest. The end of a production process is to be distinguished from the beginning of the next one by a change in expectations. It is here that Hicks's notion of equilibrium at a particular point of time is relevant. It is an equilibrium based on *ex ante* values. In a single-period theory of money, comparisons and differences with *ex post* values are disregarded. Any difference between effective and planned values is outside the scope of the analysis.

It is important to clarify that suggesting the limitation of a single-period theory of money is not to dismiss the valuable conclusions of this type of analysis. For many purposes a single-period theory is a very useful first approximation to the working of modern monetary economies. All models are simplifications of real-world problems. They omit those things which for the purpose in hand are judged to be unimportant, the purpose being to focus more clearly on the things that are retained. This also means that what is omitted and what is retained in a model is to be chosen with reference to the problem in hand. It is perfectly proper, and in fact recommended, to use one sort of model for one purpose and a different model for another purpose (Hicks 1956: 218).

Differences between *ex ante* and *ex post* values, by contrast, are the main concern of a continuation theory of money. It is here that Keynes's analysis of the non-atomistic nature of economic material, as discussed in Chapter 4, finds its full expression. Within a continuation theory of money the complex and organic nature of the interactions between the main agents of the production process, namely the central bank, commercial banks, other financial institutions, firms and households, is finally recognised. The liquidity preference of agents plays an important role in determining the quantity of money in circulation as well as the quantity of money held in portfolios. In stationary conditions, when the expectations of agents are constant (or fairly constant) and interest rates are stable (or fairly stable), the liquidity preference of, say, the central bank, commercial banks, firms and households may be safely ignored. But when these expectations are changing, the time frame assumed by the single-period theory of money becomes a less reliable guide to the analysis of circulation and holding of money. Liquidity preference is a problem of the economy over time, and if time is allowed, the choices of agents for the composition as well as the size of their portfolios come to the forefront of the analysis. In other words, the balance sheets of borrowers and lenders come to the fore, together with a rich spectrum of interest rates (Hicks 1965: 286). A continuation theory of money aims thus to explain where these interest rates lie. For this reason, the liquidity preference of savers, firms, the profit-maximising asset and liability management of banks and financial institutions, as well as the different policy reaction functions of the central bank all play a crucial role in a continuation theory of money.

Comparing these two types of dynamic analyses, it is clear that the flow equilibrium of a single period analysis of the money supply process does not come without costs for the existing stock of money. A single period equilibrium comes at the expense of disequilibrium over a sequence of periods; and this stock disequilibrium has important forward-looking implications. Any agent that is left in a state of disequilibrium will take steps to correct this disequilibrium. This is, in fact, the characteristic effect of a disequilibrium situation. It is the way in which a disequilibrium position carries its effects into the sequence of subsequent periods that is both important and interesting (Hicks 1985: 86–87; see also Hicks 1974: 36). In other words, flow and stock equilibria compete against each other, and this interaction falls outside a single period analysis, occurring instead over a sequence of single periods. It is in fact the property of a continuation analysis of the money supply process to investigate the link between the circulation of the means of payment and the holding of a liquid store of wealth. A complex theory of flows and stocks of money replaces the simple single period analysis of the money supply process. Reality thus takes the dominant role, but at the cost of the clear-cut single period analysis.

> The equilibrium conditions do not determine the actual path; all that they determine (or the most that they can determine) is an equilibrium path that we can use as a standard of reference. There will always be deviations from the equilibrium path. Some of these are simply due to imperfect planning (lack of foresight). But once a deviation has occurred, it leaves those affected in a state of stock disequilibrium; and their endeavours to right that disequilibrium are a main determinant of the next steps on the actual path. They are not the only determinant; the usual static propensities and technical restraints, all the things that are alone at work on the equilibrium path, are also present. It is, however, of the greatest importance to distinguish these two elements, which work in a distinctly different manner. The 'equilibrium' forces are (relatively) dependable; the 'disequilibrium' forces are much less dependable. We can invent rules for their working, and calculate the behaviour of the resulting models; but such calculations are of illustrative value only. This is where 'states of mind' are of dominating importance; and states of mind cannot readily be reduced to rule.
>
> (Hicks 1985: 87–88)

Conclusions

Hicks is considered a great old master of our discipline. It is often claimed that economic theory, for good or bad, has been shaped to an extraordinary degree by his writings. However, as is often the case with great masters, as time goes by, his contributions are more and more respected, but less and less read. This chapter has made a modest attempt to alter this practice, by showing that some of the writings of the early Hicks, as well as of the late and more critical Hicks, can be used to shed light on key issues discussed in previous chapters, namely the role of uncertainty, money and time in modern economic theories and methods. In particular, this chapter has explored Hicks's original distinction between a single period and a continuation theory, since this distinction is used in Chapters 7 and 8 to interpret the debate in the endogenous money theory between Horizontalists and Structuralists.

7 Horizontalist and Structuralist analyses of endogenous money

Introduction

The past two decades have seen the flourishing of a complex body of contributions in Post Keynesian economics, investigating the nature and roles of money in modern economies. The basic principle of these contributions is the idea that money has the nature of a debit–credit relationship, and it fulfils the need for a standard of value in which contractual obligations for the organisation of production and exchange activities are made (Dow and Smithin 1999: 77, also Laidler 1997: 1213–1214). As was discussed in Chapter 5, the roles of money as a final means of payment and as a store of wealth are then derived from this function on the hypothesis that economic agents interact in an environment subject to uncertainty (see Table 5.1 above).

Modern Post Keynesian contributions also maintain that money is a by-product of the normal working of the economic mechanism. Its supply arises as a result of the creation of new bank liabilities within the income generation process (Moore 1988). In other words, the stock of money in a country is determined by the demand for loans, and the latter is causally dependent upon the economic variables that affect the level of output. Because the process of money creation lies within the economic system rather than in the independent discretionary actions of the central bank, this view has been labelled endogenous money theory to distinguish it from the exogenous money theory of the Monetarist school (Cottrell 1986). Several contributions have also linked endogenous money theory to the works of Wicksell (1898), Schumpeter (1912), Keynes (1930, 1933a, 1936, 1937),[1]

---

1 Carvalho (1992), Graziani (1984, 1996), Messori (1991), Minsky (1975), Moore (1988: Ch. 8) and, especially, Dow (1997) all deal with the controversial issue of Keynes's approach to endogenous money.

Kalecki (1954),[2] Robinson (1956, 1970), and especially Kaldor (e.g. Kaldor 1970b, 1982b).[3]

This chapter discusses the main features of the endogenous money theory.[4] It starts with an analysis of the Horizontalist (also called accommodationist) approach, which historically represents the first wave of modern contributions to endogenous money theory. The Horizontalist analysis of endogenous money is based on two tenets, namely that 'loans create deposits', and 'deposits generate reserves'. These two tenets will be explored through an analysis of the balance sheets of commercial banks and the central bank.

Next, there follows an analysis of the Structuralist analysis, which has clarified and refined some features of the Horizontalist approach. This book defends the view that the Structuralist analysis is a natural development of the early Horizontalist theory of endogenous money. In fact the above-stated two original tenets of the theory are retained, but they are interpreted in the light of a more explicit consideration of the liquidity preference of the agents involved in the money supply process, namely households, firms, commercial banks and the central bank.

It is worth noting that the Structuralist interpretation of the liquidity preference theory draws explicitly on all of three major works of Keynes, namely the *General Theory* (1936), *A Treatise on Money* (Keynes 1930) and *A Treatise on Probability* (Keynes 1921), in an a clear attempt to move beyond the narrow interpretation of liquidity preference championed by Monetarists and textbook Keynesians. This generalised liquidity preference theory also demonstrates the relevance of the distinction between the notion of risk and uncertainty, discussed in Chapter 4, for a proper understanding

2 Drawing upon the recent publication of the collected works of Kalecki, Sawyer (2001a, 2001b) argues that Kalecki, too, made important, though largely ignored, contributions to endogenous money theory.

3 See, for instance, Rochon (2000), and Bertocco (2001). More generally, Realfonzo (1998) provides a comprehensive and thoughtful survey of the endogenous money theory over the first four decades of the last century. Fontana (1997) shows that the little known French economist Mireaux is also part of that long tradition.

4 A thorough and issue-related account of the endogenous money theory and its policy implications can be found in the aptly titled *A Handbook of Alternative Monetary Economics* (Arestis and Sawyer 2006). Valuable investigations into issues related to endogenous money are also provided by Arestis (1988), Bellofiore and Ferri (2001), Bibow (1998), Cottrell (1986), Dalziel (1996, 2000, 2001), Deleplace and Nell (1996), Docherty (2005), Goodhart (2002), Hewitson (1995), Howells (1995), Musella and Panico (1995), Palley (1996c) Rochon (1999a, 1999b), Rochon and Rossi (2003), Rochon and Vernengo (2001), Rossi (1998, 2001) and Smithin (2000). Critical surveys of Post Keynesian monetary economics are put forward by Cottrell (1994) and Hewitson (1995).

of the complex debit–credit relationships of households, firms, banks and the central bank in the modern monetary economies.

The Horizontalist analysis of endogenous money

Historically the Horizontalist approach was the first type of analysis in Post Keynesian economics to propose an endogenous money view. It emerged in the 1970s in the spirit of the contributions to monetary theory by Kaldor (1970b) and Weintraub (1978), who argued against Monetarist theory and policy. Later came the *magnum opus* on endogenous money by Basil Moore (1988) titled *Horizontalists and Verticalists*, where explicit reference is made to the Post Keynesian and Monetarist graphical representations of the money supply curve as a horizontal and vertical line, respectively. Therefore, one of the major contributions of the Horizontalist approach was the critical appraisal of the Monetarist analysis of money and monetary policy. According to the Monetarists, the total quantity of monetary reserves controlled by the central bank determines the total supply of bank deposits in a country. For this reason, monetary reserves are also called high-powered money or monetary base. Monetary reserves support a multiple quantity of bank deposits, which are then used by banks to make loans.[5] Once this money multiplier theory is married to the quantity theory of money, the well-known policy conclusion follows that inflation is caused by monetary overexpansion, and deflation by monetary underexpansion, or even absolute contraction, and that both problems can be prevented by proper control of the supply of monetary reserves.

The Horizontalist analysis of money rejects the Monetarist theory and its policy conclusions. It proposes an alternative theory of money and banking based on the aforementioned two major tenets, namely 'loans create deposits', and 'deposits generate reserves' (Moore 1988).[6] These two tenets can be explained through an analysis of the balance sheets of commercial banks and the central bank.[7] The use of balance sheets is crucial for highlighting the debit–credit nature of money. According to the Horizontalist analysis, money is neither a commodity nor is it 'fiat'. Money is not a commodity because its purchasing power is not determined by the intrinsic

5   See, for a rich historical account of the money multiplier theory, Realfonzo (1998).
6   Moore (1988) and Lavoie (1992) and many Horizontalists prefer the expression 'deposits make reserves'. However, in this book the latter is replaced with the expression 'deposits generate reserves' in order to distinguish it from the saying 'loans make deposits', the reason beings that behind these similar expressions there are different economic mechanisms at work.
7   The following balance sheet analysis draws on Lavoie (2003, 2006), and Godley and Lavoie (2007).

value of its material, independently of its monetary role. Money is not fiat, because it is not an asset without a matching liability.

For the sake of simplicity, the analysis of endogenous money starts with the simple case of a pure credit economy, and it draws on the monetary circuit presented in Chapter 5 (see Figure 5.1 above). In a pure credit economy there is no currency money, and all transactions between wage earners (or, more generally, households) and producers (or, more generally, firms) are made through the banking system. For the sake of simplicity, it is initially assumed that the banking system is composed of a single bank.

Table 7.1 describes the basic loans supply process in a pure credit economy. It covers stages one and two of the monetary circuit,[8] which represent the beginning of the production process. Once negotiations in the labour market between households and firms are concluded, firms need to finance their wage bill before the production process can be started. But where is the initial finance covering the wage bill to come from? According to the Horizontalist analysis of endogenous money, the answer to this question must address the fact that in the real world the production process takes time. This means that firms incur and pay production costs before sale proceeds are received. Loans are thus demanded by firms to finance their wage bill. The reason for starting with a pure credit economy is now evident. It makes transparent the process by which loans are supplied. The banking system creates *ex nihilo* loans for firms. In other words, the banking system sets the interest rate on loans, and then it accommodates all demands for loans (including overdrafts) by creditworthy borrowers. The only limit to the supply of loans is thus given by the willingness of firms to borrow, and by the willingness of the banking system to grant creditworthy status to firms.

Table 7.1 The basic loans supply process in a pure credit economy with a single bank

BANKING SYSTEM	
Assets	*Liabilities*
Loans to firms: +100	Firms deposits: +100
Loans to firms: +100	Households deposits: +100

8 For obvious reasons of space, the representation of the remaining stages of the monetary circuit through an analysis of the balance sheets of commercial banks and the central bank cannot be pursued here. The interested reader is referred to Lavoie (1992: 152–165), where a full representation of the monetary circuit via the balance sheets of banks and the central bank is presented.

As Table 7.1, row 1, shows, at the simple stroke of a pen the banking system records loans to creditworthy firms for £100 (e.g. million) on its assets side, and £100 (e.g. million) deposits of firms on its liabilities side. These deposits are then used by firms to pay households wages and salaries for their labour services. Thus, Table 7.1, row 2, shows that the ownership of deposits is transferred from firms to households. Notwithstanding the issue of the ownership of the newly created deposits, the analysis of the loans supply process confirms the validity of the first tenet of the Horizontalist analysis, namely that loans create deposits.

Table 7.1 shows that not only do loans create deposits, but also that loans create *an equal amount* of deposits. This conclusion is derived from the analysis of the loans supply process, when the banking system is made up of a single bank. What happens if there are two or more banks operating in the economy? For the sake of simplicity, let us assume that there are only two banks or sets of banks in the economy. The first bank is a business bank (hereafter Bank B), and it specialises in making loans to firms. The second bank is a deposits bank (hereafter Bank D), and it specialises in collecting deposits from households. Table 7.2, row 1, reproduces the results of the previous analysis of the loans supply process. Once loans are supplied, and then used to pay households for their labour services, both banks making up the banking system record £100 million on their assets side, and £100 million of deposits of households on their liabilities side.

Table 7.2, row 2, records the second-round effects of the loans supply process. At the end of the transaction period, Bank B registers an outflow of deposits of households in favour of Bank D. In other words, the cheques drawn by the households customers of Bank B in favour of the households customers of Bank D exceed the cheques drawn by the customers of Bank D in favour of the customers of Bank B. From this perspective, Table 7.2, row 2, represents the extreme case, when Bank B realises that all deposits have been transferred in favour of Bank D. This means that Bank B is indebted vis-à-vis Bank D for £100 million. In the absence of a central bank, the accounts will balance only if Bank D agrees to make a direct or indirect loan for a similar amount to Bank B. In the first case, which is represented by Table 7.2, row 2, £100 million of loans are recorded on the assets side of Bank D, and £100 million of funds are recorded on the liabilities side of Bank B. In the case of an indirect loan, which is represented by Table 7.3, row 2, Bank B issues £100 million of certificates of deposits (hereafter CDs), which are bought by Bank D.[9]

---

9 Bank B could also arrange for the *securitisation* of part of its assets, i.e. it may transform part of its loans into marketable assets, and sell them to financial institutions. In this case,

Table 7.2 The basic loans supply process in a pure credit economy with two banks

BANK B		BANK D	
Assets	*Liabilities*	*Assets*	*Liabilities*
Loans to firms: +100	Households deposits: +100	Loans to firms: +100	Households deposits: +100
Loans to firms: +100	Households deposits: 0	Loans to firms: +100	Households deposits: +200
	Bank D funds: +100	Loans to Bank B: +100	

The analysis of the loans supply process with two banks or a set of banks confirms again the validity of the first tenet of the Horizontalist analysis, namely that loans create deposits. However, as Table 7.2 and Table 7.3 show, £200 million of loans create an equal amount of deposits only for the banking system as a whole. Depending on the behaviour of households, each individual bank may actually be a deposits-deficit bank or a deposits-surplus bank. In other words, for each single bank, loans do create deposits, but it is only by chance that loans create an equal amount of deposits. Yet, provided that banks agree between themselves on an appropriate interest rate on loans (Table 7.2) or on CDs (Table 7.3), their accounts will balance, and the situation represented in Tables 7.2 and 7.3 can perpetuate itself. This means that, as long as the interbank interest rate (Table 7.2) or the interest rate on CDs (Table 7.3) is set between the rate that Bank D is paying on its deposits and the rate that Bank B is charging to its borrowers, the banks do not face any liquidity problem, and their own businesses can prosper.

The second main tenet of the Horizontalist analysis of endogenous money, namely that 'deposits generate reserves' can be explained through an analysis of the balance sheets of the central bank and the other banks. This tenet is closely related to the role of the central bank as the residual supplier of liquidity to the economy. For the sake of simplicity, it is initially assumed that the banking system is again composed of one single commercial bank. Later on in the analysis, the commercial bank is again replaced by a business bank and a deposits bank.

In the pure credit economy described above, all transactions go through the books of the banking system. The simplest way of bringing the central bank into the previous analysis is to assume that not all transactions are made through the banking system. In other words, households prefer to carry out part of their daily transactions with banknotes issued by the central bank. How is the commercial bank going to get these banknotes? As in the example of a pure credit economy, the reason for starting with the case of a single commercial bank and the central bank is now evident. It makes transparent the processes by which banknotes and, as will be shown later, monetary reserves more generally, are supplied. The acceptability of bank deposits as a means of payment depends on the confidence of households that deposits can always be used for buying goods and services. This means that deposits must always be convertible into legal tender, i.e. into cash by way of banknotes and coins, on demand. Therefore, whenever households want to

---

Bank B moves some assets off its balance sheet. This is an attractive way to avoid capital losses or to escape capital requirements. This possibility is discussed later in the chapter, after the different roles of banks and financial institutions are fully explored.

Table 7.3 The basic loans supply process with two banks and certificate of deposits

	BANK B		BANK D	
Assets	*Liabilities*	*Assets*	*Liabilities*
Loans to firms: +100	Households deposits: +100	Loans to firms: +100	Households deposits: +100
Loans to firms: +100	Households deposits: 0	Loans to firms: +100	Households deposits: +200
	CDs: +100	CDs: +100	

have deposits transformed into cash, the commercial bank must borrow reserves from the central bank. Table 7.4 shows the balance sheets of the commercial bank and the central bank.

Table 7.4, row 1, reproduces the results of the previous analysis of the loans supply process with a single bank (see Table 7.1 above). The effects of the choice of households between deposits and cash are also recorded in Table 7.4. Since households now demand £10 million of deposits to be converted into cash, the commercial bank must borrow this amount of cash from the central bank. Table 7.4, row 2, shows that £10 million of loans are recorded on the assets side of the central bank, and £10 million of cash are recorded on the liabilities side of the commercial bank. The analysis in Table 7.4 together with the previous analyses clarifies the role of trust, confidence and creditworthiness in the Horizontalist analysis of endogenous money. Banks grant loans to firms as long as they trust them to repay their debts. Similarly, households are content to leave deposits at the banks as long as they have total confidence that they can convert them into cash on demand and, more generally, draw on these deposits at will for buying goods and services. Trust, confidence and credit-worthiness, therefore, play a key role in the Horizontalist analysis of the monetary system (Lavoie 1992: Ch. 4, 2003).

In the previous example, it became evident that the central bank has a very important role in the Horizontalist analysis of endogenous money. The central bank is the issuer of cash, i.e. it is the supplier of legal tender in the economy. As long as households demand legal tender in the economy, the commercial bank is forced to go into debt with the central bank. This conclusion reveals the more general role of the central bank. According to the Horizontalist analysis of endogenous money, the central bank is not only the supplier of legal tender in the economy, but more generally it is the residual supplier of liquidity (i.e. cash) to the economic system. Tables 7.5 and 7.6 highlight this role of the central bank. They describe the basic reserves supply process in the case of a single bank, and two banks or a set of banks, respectively.

Table 7.5, row 1, reproduces the results of the previous analysis of the loans supply process with a single bank (see Table 7.1 above). For the sake of simplicity, let us assume that households do not demand cash, i.e. households are content to have all transactions going through the books of the banking system. The commercial bank is thus not forced to go into debt with the central bank. What is the role, if any, of the central bank in this situation? The Horizontalist analysis of endogenous money maintains that the central bank plays a crucial role in the economy, independently of the existence of a demand for cash. The reason for this is that the commercial bank voluntarily demands legal tender to maintain the general acceptability

Table 7.4 The basic loans supply process with banknotes

COMMERCIAL BANK

Assets	Liabilities
Loans to firms: +100	Households deposits: +100
Loans to firms: +100	Households deposits: +90
	Banknotes: +10

CENTRAL BANK

Assets	Liabilities
Commercial bank loans: +10	Commercial bank deposits: +10

Table 7.5 The basic reserves supply process with one commercial bank

COMMERCIAL BANK

Assets	Liabilities
Loans to firms: +100	Households deposits: +100
Loans to firms: +100	Households deposits: +100
Reserves: +10	Central bank funds: +10

CENTRAL BANK

Assets	Liabilities
Commercial bank loans: +10	Commercial bank deposits: +10

of bank deposits. In other words, whether or not households actually request deposits to be transformed into cash, the commercial bank knows that the acceptability of its bank deposits as a means of payment depends on the confidence of households that deposits can always be converted into cash for buying goods and services. This means that the commercial bank must demand monetary reserves, i.e. cash, from the central bank in order to maintain a certain desired level of monetary reserves to deposits ratio.[10] Table 7.5, row 2, shows that, for instance, £10 million of loans are recorded on the assets side of the central bank, while £10 million of central bank funds are recorded on the liabilities side of the commercial bank. In other words, monetary reserves are supplied on demand by the central bank in order to safeguard the acceptability of bank deposits as a means of payment. More generally, the central bank accommodates the liquidity needs of the commercial bank, be they banknotes or monetary reserves, in order to maintain trust and confidence in the working of the monetary system. Advocates of the Horizontalist analysis of endogenous money also maintain that, where the central bank has absolutely no choice but to accommodate the request of the commercial bank, to do otherwise would lead to a failure of public confidence and a consequent breakdown of the financial system and possibly of the whole economy, it sets the short-run nominal interest rate at which monetary reserves are lent to the commercial bank. This interest rate is the short-run interest rate used by the commercial bank to administer its own lending and deposits rates. It is an exogenous variable, in the sense that the central bank has total discretion over its level. The central bank fixes the short-run interest rate in accordance with its political or economic objectives, such as the achievement of a particular target rate of inflation (Fontana 2006).

Table 7.6 is a slightly amended version of Table 7.2 and Table 7.3 above. As in the previous cases, there are two banks or sets of banks in the economy, namely a business bank (Bank B) and a deposit bank (Bank D). However, in this case there is also a central bank operating in the economy. As in the previous situation, Bank B and Bank D grant loans to firms. These loans create an equal amount of deposits, which are then used by firms to pay households wages for their labour services. Table 7.6, row 1, shows that Bank B and Bank D both have £100 million of loans on their assets sides,

---

10 In many countries, including Australia, Canada, New Zealand, Sweden and Switzerland there are no compulsory reserves, and commercial banks in these countries hold a very low level of free reserves. This situation is the result of the particular operating procedures of the banking system, the so-called channel system (Woodford 2002: 89), which makes it easier for the central bank to provide the required daily level of reserves on demand.

Table 7.6 The basic reserves supply process with two commercial banks

BANK B

Assets	Liabilities
Loans to firms: +100	Households deposits: +100
Loans to firms: +100	Households deposits: +40
	Central bank funds: +60

BANK D

Assets	Liabilities
Loans to firms: +100	Households deposits: +100
Loans to firms: +100	Households deposits: +160
Central bank funds: +60	

CENTRAL BANK

Assets	Liabilities
Loans to Bank B: +60	Bank D deposits: +60

and £100 million of deposits of households on their liabilities sides. Table 7.6, row 2, shows that Bank B experiences an outflow of deposits towards Bank D, though this time the outflow is not as extreme as in Table 7.2 or Table 7.3. The cheques drawn by the customers of Bank B in favour of the customers of Bank D exceed by £60 million the cheques drawn by the customers of Bank D in favour of the customers of Bank B. How are Bank B and Bank D going to balance their accounts? Table 7.2 and Table 7.3 present the case where Bank D makes a direct or indirect loan to Bank B. Table 7.6, row 2, describes another more general possibility, namely that the central bank acts as the clearing house between Bank D and Bank B. In other words, the central bank is the counterpart of the required lending and borrowing operations of Bank B and Bank D, respectively. Then, Table 7.6, row 2, records £60 million of central bank funds on the liabilities side of Bank B, and £60 million of central bank funds on the assets side of Bank D. Provided that there is only a small interest rate difference between the penalty rate charged by the central bank on the funds lent to Bank B, and the deposit rate offered by the central bank on the surplus deposits borrowed from Bank D, there are no incentives for the banks to agree on a direct or indirect loan. In conclusion, this simple analysis of the reserve supply process explains the crucial role of the central bank as the residual supplier of liquidity to the economic system, and hence it confirms the validity of the second tenet of the Horizontalist analysis, namely that 'bank deposits generate reserves'.

The Structuralist analysis of endogenous money

Starting with Pollin (1991), in recent decades several Post Keynesian economists have tried to clarify and refine some of the early Horizontalist analyses of endogenous money. One of the major features of these early analyses was their bold criticism of Monetarist theory and policy. For this reason, most of the Horizontalist analyses used a dualistic approach when discussing the working of the markets for loans and monetary reserves: the central bank and the commercial banks are price-makers and quantity-takers in the monetary reserves and the loans markets, respectively. Therefore, the supply of monetary reserves and the supply of loans were best represented by horizontal lines. Any other diagrammatic representation was considered to be a misinterpretation of endogenous money theory, and an endorsement of the Monetarist theory. This meant that any argument that could be remotely associated with the Monetarist theory was excluded from endogenous money theory.

This is, in part, understandable. Horizontalist scholars like Kaldor and Moore had to present an original theory of money to a very unreceptive audience.[11] On this point, it is worth remembering that both advocates and opponents of the Monetarist theory, Kaldor being a notable exception, had relied for their arguments on an exogenous money regime, namely on the view that the central bank was able to control the rate of growth of the money supply. In other words, the notion of endogenous money was extraneous to Monetarists and textbook Keynesians alike. For this reason, early endogenous money analyses were very prescriptive and dogmatic in their statements.

One of the theories initially excluded from early endogenous money analyses was the liquidity preference theory: 'if we regard money as an endogenous factor, liquidity preference and the assumption of interest elasticity of the demand for money ceases to be of any importance' (Kaldor as quoted in Lavoie 1992: 193, see also Kaldor 1982b: 26, Moore 1988: 195–199, Rochon 2000). Therefore, it is not accidental that in their attempts to clarify and refine the contributions of the Horizontalist approach, Structuralists placed liquidity preference theory at the centre of their analysis of endogenous money. As a result, liquidity preference theory soon became one of the most contentious arguments in endogenous money theory.

Whereas Structuralists took Horizontalist scholars like Kaldor to task for downplaying the role of liquidity preference in endogenous money theory, they acknowledged the need to move beyond the narrow interpretation of liquidity preference championed by Monetarists and textbook Keynesians alike. According to Structuralists, liquidity preference theory should not be restricted to the demand for non-interest bearing money. At the minimum, liquidity preference should account for the difference between interest rates on liquid and less liquid assets. In this regard, Structuralists argued for an interpretation of the simplified liquidity preference theory proposed by Keynes in the *General Theory* (1936) in the light of the extensive monetary analysis of *A Treatise on Money* (Keynes 1930) and the early philosophical work in *A Treatise on Probability* (Keynes 1921) (Dow and Dow 1989, Dow 2006). The standard liquidity preference theory was slowly transformed into an analysis of the complex debit–credit relationships of households, firms, banks and the central bank (Wray 1995, Bell 2003). This generalised liquidity preference theory was then used as a valuable tool for explaining the particular nature and evolution of these relationships in a world of

11 Kaldor, more than anyone else on either side of the Atlantic, fought vigorously against monetarism. He had the courage of his convictions to use every means at his disposal to expose the failings of monetarism in the public domain (letters to *The Times*, speeches in the House of Lords, as well as books and journal articles), at a time when monetarism was at its zenith (it was established British Government policy under Margaret Thatcher from 1979), until his death in 1986.

uncertainty, rather than in a world of risk,[12] as is the case in the standard theory of liquidity preference (e.g. Dow 1996b, 2006, Bibow 1998, 2006).

From this perspective, the Structuralist analysis is thus a natural development of the early Horizontalist theory of endogenous money. The two original tenets of the theory, namely that 'loans create deposits' and 'deposits generate reserves', are retained. However, they are now interpreted in the light of a more explicit consideration of the liquidity preference of the agents involved in the money supply process, namely households, firms, banks and the central bank. For this reason, this chapter concludes this overview of endogenous money theory with an analysis of the liquidity preference behaviour of households, firms, banks and the central bank.

The liquidity preference of the household sector

The liquidity preference of households affects the Horizontalist analysis of the money supply process in two ways, namely through changes in both the composition and the size of their portfolios. The former amounts to a redistribution of the liquidity existing in the economy, whereas the latter leads to the creation of new means of payment. Changes in the composition of the portfolios of households affect the profitability of firms, and in this way indirectly influence the money supply process: when households' liquidity preference is low, they are more willing to exchange cash and other very liquid assets for medium- and long-term financial assets, which are offered by firms, among others. Bearing in mind the monetary circuit discussed in previous chapters (see Figure 5.1 above), this means that firms will be able to withdraw existing liquidity from the market, and use it in order to reduce their debts to the banking system. This should also help to increase the creditworthiness of firms, and therefore their bargaining power in future negotiations with the banking system.

Changes in the size of the portfolios of households directly affect the money supply process described above: when their liquidity preference falls, households are more willing to negotiate bank loans in order to finance the purchases of commodities like consumer durables or houses. In this case, the existing amount of liquidity in the economy increases. Empirical studies lend increasing support to this scenario. In the last two decades, the demand for loans by households has grown substantially and, in the case of some countries, has outstripped the total amount of lending to firms and financial institutions. For instance, in the case of the UK the last two decades have seen a continuing expansion of consumer loans, such that now the total

---

12 See, on this distinction, Chapter 4 above.

supply of loans depends more upon the behaviour of households than on the behaviour of firms (Arestis and Howells 1999).

The liquidity preference of the business sector

Another avenue of influence of liquidity preference upon the Horizontalist analysis of the money supply process works through the balance sheets of firms. As in the case of households, the liquidity preference of firms leads either to a redistribution of liquidity or to the creation of new liquidity in the economy. In the first case, the money supply process described above is only slightly affected. Some firms may now grow at their own pace, rather than follow the behaviour of other firms: when their liquidity preference is low, firms are more willing to exchange liquid assets for less liquid assets. This means that some firms may exchange cash and other liquid financial assets for capital goods produced by other firms. Similarly, firms may exchange liquid assets for long-run financial assets offered by other firms. This redistribution of liquidity between firms helps to maintain equilibrium in the balance sheets of firms with different propensities to investment.

The liquidity preference of firms may also lead to the creation of new liquidity: when their liquidity preference is low, *ceteris paribus* firms are willing to negotiate loans with the banking system in order to finance the production of new goods and services. This is the case represented in Table 7.1 above. At the other extreme, when their liquidity preference is high, regardless of the lending policy of the banking system, firms adopt a more conservative borrowing behaviour. In the case of high economic instability, low profitability and an uncertain future, some firms may even decide on an 'opt-out' strategy, reducing or suspending the flow of production, and behaving more like financial intermediaries (Bibow 1998: 251).

The liquidity preference of the commercial bank sector

The liquidity preference of banks has been the argument used *par excellence* by Structuralists to defend and extend the significance of the liquidity preference theory to the Horizontalist analysis of endogenous money (Dow 1996a). Banks play a crucial role in the money supply process. They create liquidity when they accommodate the demand for loans of firms (see, for instance, Table 7.1). They also automatically redistribute liquidity in the economy when they allow households to exchange their deposits against financial assets (see, also, Tables 7.2 and 7.3 above, which show that banks can specialise in their own business and deposits activities without facing liquidity problems). Whether they create or redistribute liquidity, the liquidity preference of banks influences the money supply process described above.

Table 7.7, row 1, reproduces the basic result of the Horizontalist analysis of the loans supply process in the more general case, when the banking system has its own funds. Once loans are supplied, and then used to pay households for their labour services, the commercial bank records £100 million of loans to firms on its assets side, and £100 million of deposits of households on its liabilities side. However, this time the profits of the commercial bank are explicitly taken into consideration. The commercial bank is in the business of making loans and managing deposits. Like any other firm, it must face the costs of buying equipment and paying wages and salaries to its employees. How is the commercial bank going to pay for these costs and make a profit for its owners? The commercial bank sets the differential between the loans rate paid by its borrowers and the deposits rate paid to its customers (on the top of any other service charges), such that in normal times its costs are covered, and the target rate of return on its own capital is achieved, net of any loss due to loans defaults.

Let us assume that the rate of interest on loans is 10 per cent and the rate of interest on deposits is 5 per cent. Assuming that firms make no interest rate payments or reimburse loans, Table 7.7, row 2, records the end-of-year outcome of the loans supply process. The commercial bank records £110 million of loans to firms on its assets side, and £105 million of household deposits, together with £5 million of own funds, on its liabilities side. The £5 million of own funds are the net worth of the commercial bank.

Table 7.7 The loans supply process and the liquidity preference of a commercial bank

COMMERCIAL BANK	
Assets	*Liabilities*
Loans to firms: +100 (1 + 0.10)	Households deposits: +100 (1 + 0.05)
	Own funds: +100 (0.10 − 0.05)
Loans to firms: +110	Households deposits: +105
	Own funds: +5
Old loans to firms: +110	Old households deposits: +105
New loans to firms: +100	New households deposits: + 100
	Own funds: +5

They are a liability of the commercial bank to its owners, which are used whenever firms default on loans.

Table 7.7, row 3, shows the role of the liquidity preference of the commercial bank in the loans supply process. As in the previous cases, the reason for considering a single commercial bank operating in a pure credit economy is now evident. It makes clear the meaning of liquidity for the banking system. In a pure credit economy there are no safe assets like monetary reserves and government bonds, except the own funds of the commercial bank. The liquidity of the balance sheet of the commercial bank is thus inversely related to the degree of risk of its assets compared to its own funds, namely the loans to own funds ratio. Table 7.7, row 2, shows that the loans to own funds ratio of the commercial bank is equal to £(110/5) million. Let us now assume that firms decide to increase the production of goods and services, and the negotiations between firms and the commercial bank are successfully concluded. The commercial bank then records £100 million of new loans to creditworthy firms on its assets side, and £100 million of new deposits of firms on its liabilities side. Firms then use these deposits to pay households for their services. At the end of the new loans supply process, Table 7.7, row 3, shows that the commercial bank records a total of £210 million of loans to firms on its assets side, and a total of £205 million of household deposits, together with £5 million of own funds, on its liabilities side. The results represented in Table 7.7, row 3, lend support to the Structuralist analysis of endogenous money: when the commercial bank grants the new set of loans, the ratio of loans to own funds rises to £(210/5) million. In other words, as the commercial bank expands its lending activity, its liquidity is automatically reduced. This outcome may affect the price and availability of new loans negotiated by the commercial bank in future. For this reason, Structuralists maintain that the liquidity preference of the banking system is an integral part of the analysis of the money supply process.

The liquidity preference of the central bank

Finally, the theory of liquidity preference could be usefully extended to the role of the central bank in the money supply process described above. In this case, Structuralists argue that the central bank is not passive in the face of the demand for reserves of banks, but instead it makes active lending decisions in accordance with its main objective of maintaining an orderly and efficient banking system (Dow and Rodríguez-Fuentes 1998, Sawyer 1996). In other words, the role of the central bank in the money supply process described above is not to do what commercial banks ask it to do, for instance passively accommodate their demand for reserves, but rather to do what is in the interest of the economy as a whole. This means that depending on the circumstances, the central bank may decide to change the price of monetary reserves in response to, among other things, the behaviour of the banking system and the state of the economy, especially with regard to the actual rate of inflation vis-à-vis the central bank's target rate of inflation, if it has one.

The concept of liquidity preference for the central bank builds on the Horizontalist analysis of the central bank as the residual supplier of liquidity to the economy. The central bank controls the short-run interest rate, namely the base rate used by the banking system to set all lending and borrowing rates. Therefore, when the central bank changes the short-run rate (e.g. the federal funds rate in the US, or the repo rate in the UK), it affects the cost of obtaining monetary reserves and, by doing so, may influence the interest on loans charged by the banking system (Palley 1991, Niggle 1991).

Conclusions

An overview of the main features of the Horizontalist and Structuralist analyses of endogenous money has been provided in this chapter. It started with the study of the balance sheets of banks and the central bank in a pure credit economy, which was used to shed light on the main contributions of the Horizontalist analysis, including the debit–credit nature of money, the 'loans create deposits' tenet, as well as the 'deposits generate reserves' tenet. Then the Structuralist analysis was discussed. This approach has been presented as a further historical development of the Horizontalist analysis of endogenous money. The Structuralist analysis has retained the main contributions of the Horizontalist analysis, including the 'loans create deposits' and 'deposits generate reserves' tenets, but it has interpreted them in the light of a more explicit consideration of the liquidity preference of the agents involved in the money supply process, namely households, firms, commercial banks and the central bank.

Many of the endogenous money propositions discussed in this chapter, including the debit–credit nature of money, and the 'loans create deposits' and 'deposits generate reserves' tenets are further examined in Chapter 8, where it is argued that today it is not fruitful to view the Horizontalist and Structuralist analyses of endogenous money as being in opposition to each other. Instead, Chapter 8 uses Hicks's original distinction, considered in Chapter 6, between a single period and a continuation analysis to discuss similarities and differences between the two analyses of endogenous money presented in this chapter. The main objective of Chapter 8 is thus to explain the complementary nature of the Horizontalist and Structuralist analyses, and their roles within a more general theory of endogenous money.

8 A general theory of endogenous money

Introduction

In Chapter 7 it was argued that one of the major contributions in Post Keynesian economics is the theory of endogenous money: the supply of money is determined by the demand for loans, and the latter originates within the economic system in order to finance the production and accumulation processes, consumer expenditure (especially on durable goods), or the upsurge of speculative purchases. The main policy implication of this theory is that money and monetary policy are not neutral either in the short or the long run: money is needed for, and is the purpose of, financing the core activities of capitalist economies. While these propositions are now widely accepted by most, if not all, Post Keynesian economists and more generally by heterodox economists,[1] there are several details in the theory of endogenous money that are still contentious.[2] The debate between proponents of the Horizontalist (or accommodationist) analysis and those of the Structuralist analysis of endogenous money is based around the following three controversies. First, there is disagreement over the degree of accommodation by central banks of the demand for reserves by commercial banks. Are central

---

1 In the last couple of decades the economic profession at large has converged towards the view that the money supply is endogenous, though this view is grounded more on historical than theoretical arguments, as in the Post Keynesian tradition. This means that should historical circumstances change, such as the money demand function becoming stable again, the economic profession may support once more the Monetarist theory of exogenous money, together with its deleterious policy implications. See, on the meaning and nature of the endogenous money theory in Post Keynesian economics and monetary economics more generally, Fontana (2007) and Fontana and Palacio-Vera (2002: 557–559, 2004).

2 For critical surveys of the Post Keynesian theory of endogenous money, see Cottrell (1994), Dalziel (2001: Ch. 3), Dow (2006), Fontana (2003b), Fontana and Realfonzo (2005), Hein (2008, Part II), Hewitson (1995), Howells (1995), Lavoie (2006), Rochon (1999b) and Rochon and Rossi (2003).

banks always willing to supply the required reserves at the going short-run nominal interest rate? Or could they attempt to resist this demand by changing this interest rate? Second, there is a dispute about the meaning and relevance of the liquidity preference of commercial banks. Is liquidity preference theory consistent with endogenous money? And, if so, does this mean that there is an upward sloping supply curve for loans? Thirdly, there is a controversy over the implications of the liquidity preference of the non-bank private sector. Are the preferences of the final recipients of bank deposits (e.g. wage earners) necessarily consistent with the preferences of the first recipients of these deposits (e.g. firms)? And, if not, is there a mechanism that reconciles the different preferences?

The objectives of this chapter are twofold. The first objective is to review these controversial issues debated by Horizontalists and Structuralists with the help of an original four-panel diagram (Fontana 2003b). The Horizontalist and Structuralist analyses of endogenous money provide insightful perspectives on the ways central banks, commercial banks, firms, financial intermediaries, and wage earners enter into the money supply process. Unfortunately, as explained in the previous chapter, these perspectives are often presented in a dualistic style, with readers urged to support either the Horizontalist or the Structuralist analyses (e.g. Lavoie 2006). The simple graphical analysis proposed in this chapter moves beyond this dualistic view of endogenous money, by presenting simply and concisely the nature and origin of the differences between Horizontalists and Structuralists.

The second objective of this chapter is to bring into play the encompassing principle discussed in Chapter 2. Having presented the differences between the Horizontalist and the Structuralist analyses, in the second part of this chapter the domains of relevance of these analyses are extended by encompassing them in a more general theory of endogenous money. This general theory is grounded on Hicks's distinction between a single period analysis and a continuation analysis. As discussed in Chapter 6, the former aims to portray simple and stable relationships that abstract from real-world complexities. For this reason, a single period analysis is based on the tacit assumption that within any period considered economic agents hold constant expectations, and it then explains the sequential stages of the money supply process. However, one of the key features of the money supply process is the possibility of affecting the expectations of all agents involved in it. Therefore, the causes and effects of changes in the state of expectations of central banks, commercial banks, firms, financial intermediaries and wage earners are the main concern of a continuation analysis.

Controversial issues

The core argument of endogenous money theory is that the money supply is determined by the demand for loans, and the latter originates within the economic system in order to finance the production and accumulation processes, consumer expenditure or an upsurge of speculative purchases. This means that any representation of endogenous money theory requires at the minimum three markets and four types of economic agents, namely a central bank, commercial banks (banks for short), firms and wage earners. In the following, the debate between Horizontalists and Structuralists is therefore presented in terms of the controversial arguments surrounding the behaviour of these economic agents in the market for monetary reserves, the credit or loans market and the financial markets, respectively.

The market for monetary reserves

The first controversy between Horizontalists and Structuralists is over the relationship between the central bank and the commercial banks. In endogenous money theory, central banks set the short-run nominal interest rate (e.g. the federal funds rate in USA and the official bank rate in the UK), and they then supply monetary reserves on demand in exchange for acceptable collateral. The short-run nominal interest rate is thus the control-instrument used by central banks to influence the price of credit, and thus the level of bank lending. For instance, changes in the short-run nominal interest rate prompt banks to modify their base rates (e.g. personal loan rates and mortgage rates) at which they lend to their customers. These rates, *ceteris paribus*, have an important role in influencing the levels of investment and consumption, and hence the level of aggregate demand, which in turn affects the volume of output and employment.

The differences between the two analyses of endogenous money can be introduced in terms of a short-run reaction function measuring the elasticity of the nominal interest rate with respect to changes in the demand for reserves. Horizontalists argue for an infinitely elastic reaction function in the time period between revisions of the short-run nominal interest rate (e.g. Moore 1991, 1995), whereas Structuralists defend a less than perfectly elastic function (e.g. Pollin 1991).

The four-panel diagram in Figure 8.1 shows the contentious description of the market for reserves.[3] The focus of the analysis is upon flows, namely changes in the supply of money, and how these changes arise from the flow

---

3   The author is indebted to Dow (1996a, 1997), Howells (1995), Lavoie (1996), Palley (1994, 1996b), Pollin (1996) and Sawyer (1996) for early representations of a similar diagram.

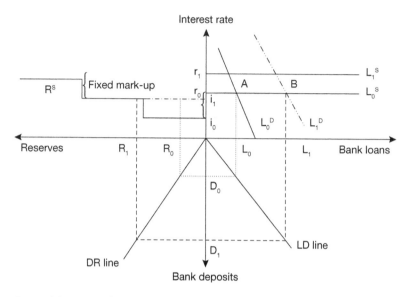

Figure 8.1 A general endogenous money analysis of the reserve market

of new bank loans to borrowers. The upper left panel portrays the market for reserves. The supply of reserves is represented by a step function, with each horizontal segment representing a different interest rate policy (e.g. i_0, i_1). The horizontal parts of the schedule show the accommodative behaviour on the part of the central bank, while the upward stepwise trend (from right to left in the diagram) reflects the Structuralist view that central banks have a less than perfectly elastic reaction function. The upper right panel portrays the credit market, where banks and firms negotiate terms and conditions for the supply of new loans. Since the debate over the slope of the supply curve of loans is postponed to the next section, the curve is represented by a perfectly elastic schedule at a base rate (e.g. r_0), determined as a fixed mark-up over the short-run nominal interest rate (e.g. i_0) set by the central bank. The demand for loans (e.g. L_0^D) is a decreasing function of the base rate (r), and together with the supply of loans (e.g. L_0^S), it determines the total volume of credit (e.g. L_0).

The lower panels are used to describe two main tenets of the endogenous money theory, namely 'loans create deposits' (*LD* or loans–deposits line), and 'deposits generate reserves' (*DR* or deposits–reserves line), respectively. The equilibrium in the credit market determines via the *LD* line the supply of new deposits (e.g. D_0) in the lower right panel. Note that the *LD* line represents the balance sheet constraint of banks and, for the sake of making the graphical exposition feasible, it is drawn on the assumption that banks hold their liabilities, like time or demand deposits, in a given proportion. The supply of reserves (e.g. R_0) associated with the supply of new bank deposits (e.g. D_0) is shown via the DR line in the lower left panel. The DR line represents the total demand for reserves.

The four-panel diagram illustrates the underlying sequential analysis that characterises endogenous money theory, as well as the controversial issues related to the reaction function of the central bank. Expansionary shifts of the demand for bank loans (e.g. L_1^D) cause, via the LD line and the DR line, increases in the level of bank deposits (e.g. D_1), and of reserves (e.g. R_1), respectively. But, as a result of the new higher level of reserves, the central bank might, though it does not need to, decide to tighten conditions in the market for reserves by moving to an (i_1) interest rate policy. This change in the policy stance of the central bank is then likely to affect the lending policy of banks in the credit market (e.g. L_1^S).

Note that the graphical representation of the supply of monetary reserves is not inconsistent with the neo-Chartalist view that most of the central bank actions are defensive in nature and are mainly undertaken in order to smooth out the imbalances in the pattern of money flows between the Government's accounts, on the one hand, and the banks, on the other (Wray 1998: Ch. 5, also Lavoie 2006). The central bank supplies the reserves which the banking system as a whole needs in order to achieve balance by the end of each settlement day. However, at any time the central bank sets the price of these reserves, and hence it can change the price, if it considers it appropriate or necessary to do so.

Furthermore, it is necessary to reiterate the importance for banks of the reserve market compared to the wholesale market (see, for a different view, Dow 2006: 46). It is only in the former that liquidity is created, whereas the role of the latter is to circulate existing liquidity between banks. The infamous run on Northern Rock, the fifth-biggest mortgage lender in Britain, in September 2007 is a case in point (*Economist* 2007). When on the back of problems in the sub-prime mortgage market in the USA, British banks increased their liquidity preference and avoided lending to each other on the wholesale market, Northern Rock was unable to refinance its business. The Bank of England did not intervene by providing the much needed new liquidity, and panic spread. Whatever the evaluation of the behaviour of the Bank of England, it is clear that, beyond normal circumstances, only the central bank can save a bank from illiquidity. The central bank is the bank to the banking system, i.e. as was explained in Chapter 7, the central bank performs a pivotal role as the lender of last resort to the banking system, and thus as the residual supplier of liquidity to the economy as a whole. The reserve market is still relevant for the money supply process, though many countries including Canada, Sweden, Australia and New Zealand now have no compulsory reserve requirements.

More generally, this simple example suggests that central banks have a crucial role in the money supply process. By adjusting the short-run nominal interest rate, they are able to affect lending conditions in the credit market and, more generally, to determine the cost and availability of liquidity throughout the economy. This power of central banks is recognised by both Horizontalists (e.g. Lavoie 1992: 186–189) and Structuralists (e.g. Howells 1995: 12–17). Their main difference lies in the assumptions regarding the state of expectations of central banks during the money supply process. Horizontalists discuss the supply curve of reserves associated with a constant state of expectations, whereas Structuralists allow for the effects of changes in the state of expectations. Therefore, while the former prefer to discriminate between different stances of monetary policy and focus only on the freely managed short-run nominal interest rate stance (Lavoie 1996: 279, Moore 1983: 265, n. 9), the latter are more inclined to consider complex reaction functions of central banks (Wray 1992: 307, Palley 1996a: 592–593). In terms of Figure 8.1, by the particular temporal nature of their models, Structuralists tend to consider the overall upward sloping step function representing the supply of reserves (i.e. R^S), whereas Horizontalists focus on each single horizontal part of it (i.e. either i_0 or i_1 policy line).

The credit market

A more controversial argument between Horizontalists and Structuralists is over the behaviour of banks in the credit or loans market. Whether or not reserves are forthcoming at a constant short-run nominal interest rate, Structuralists hold that, as a result of an increase in lending activity, price and non-price terms of credit would tend to rise. Price terms are base interest rates like the standard mortgage rate, whereas non-price terms refer mainly to the income and assets collateral requirements (Wolfson 1996: 456–457).

Drawing on Minsky's analysis of corporate financial behaviour (Minsky 1975: Chs 5 and 6), most Structuralists argue that banks raise their base interest rates at the peak of the business cycle (e.g. Wray 1995: 278–280).[4] As lending grows, banks become increasingly concerned about their own portfolio balance (usually measured by the ratio of loans to equity and the

---

4 Recently, some Structuralists have accepted that this need not necessarily be the case (e.g. Howells 1995: 20, Dow 2006: 46). For instance, they acknowledge the point made by Lavoie (1996: 285–290) to the effect that over the business cycle, loans are being taken out, profits earned and loans repaid (out of profits, and out of borrowing), such that the ratio of loans to profits or to equity does not necessarily rise during the business upswing.

ratio of loans to safe assets), as well as the liquidity level of their customers (usually indicated by the ratio of debt to equity of firms). Similarly, Structuralists maintain that in these circumstances banks often impose restrictions on their lending activity. They conclude that if price and non-price terms are properly considered, the supply of loans is best represented by an upward sloping curve (Dow 1996a: 498–504, 2006: 43–49).

For their part, Horizontalists argue for a horizontal supply curve in the interest–loans space. However, they acknowledge that banks may impose quantitative restrictions on their customers (Moore 1988: 24). Similarly, Horizontalists accept that the liquidity ratios of banks and customers play a role in determining base rates over the business cycle. However, they refute the contention that the supply of loans is necessarily upward sloping in the long run (Lavoie 1996: 286 and 289, 2006: 23). Horizontalists prefer to discuss the effects of changing liquidity ratios in terms of initial restrictions on the borrowing activity of customers. They argue that banks do not curtail credit by marginal variations of the mark-up, though they do change over time the requirements for the identification of creditworthy customers (non-price terms for new loans) and the base rate of their credit offer (price terms for new loans). Therefore, at all times banks only accommodate creditworthy applicants or, in other words, the *effective* demand for loans. More importantly, the supply of loans is a truncated horizontal line: beyond some point, the supply curve simply vanishes (Lavoie 1996: 288). Changed conditions in the credit market are thus best represented by a shift in the demand curve and a new horizontal supply curve.

Figure 8.2 shows the differences between the Horizontalist and Structuralist analyses of the credit or loans market. The significant difference from Figure 8.1 is the assumption, made in order to simplify the analysis, of a perfectly elastic schedule for the supply of reserves. This means that only a single monetary policy stance is considered (e.g. an i_0 interest rate policy). More importantly, the loans supply schedule is now a function of the liquidity ratios of banks and their customers. During an economic expansion banks are probably going to experience a reduction in the level of liquidity. Illiquidity comes from increasingly risky new loans, and from outstanding loans being perceived as more risky. As the peak of the cycle is approached, some banks become aware of the objective fragility of the system and anxious about the illiquidity of their balance sheets. They are then likely to tighten the requirements for new credit and to raise their base rates (e.g. r_1). Similarly, as customers take on more debt, banks become concerned about the solvency of their borrowers. As in the previous case, it is likely that banks would revise their lending requirements upwards, and raise the base rates (e.g. r_1). Thus, in these circumstances the supply of loans (L^S) is better represented by a step function. Banks set their base rate, and this determines

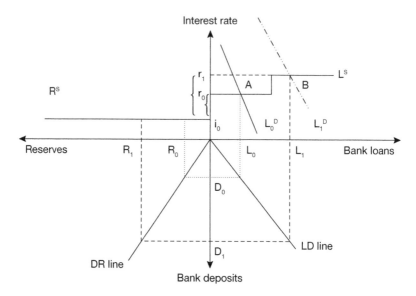

Figure 8.2 A general endogenous money analysis of the credit market

the height of the loans supply curve (i.e. the relevant horizontal line of the L^S). Their perception of the state of the economy explains the length of the horizontal parts of the curve, i.e. how long banks hold constant the supply price of loans (Fontana 2003b).

In short, one of the main differences between the Horizontalist and Structuralist analyses of endogenous money lies in the different assumptions about the behaviour of banks in the credit market. Horizontalists analyse the credit market on the assumption that during the money supply process banks are not affected by changes, if any, in their own liquidity ratios, and the liquidity ratios of their customers. Structuralists allow for the possibility that over the business cycle banks revise price and non-price terms of credit.

The financial markets

Another controversy between Horizontalists and Structuralists is related to the relationship between the different recipients of deposits. In the previous chapter it was argued that the demand for loans originates mainly with firms,[5]

---

5 The previous chapters have also argued that lending patterns vary from one country to another, and evolve over time, as is the case in the UK where most bank lending in recent years has been to households.

while the deposits created by this lending are eventually held by wage earners. Firms are deficit units involved in income–expenditure decisions. They negotiate with banks the amount of loans necessary for purchasing capital and labour services, and once collateral requirements are satisfied, they own the resulting deposits. These deposits are then exchanged with the owners of the inputs necessary for the production process, in return for their capital and labour services. If transactions between firms are ignored, i.e. if the purchasing of capital services is considered an internal transaction of the business sector, labour services are the only inputs they buy. The supply of new loans is therefore equal to the flow of new deposits transferred from firms to wage earners.

Wage earners use these bank deposits to buy goods and services in the goods market and securities in the financial markets. In the simple case in which the public sector and the foreign sector are ignored, firms issue all securities available for purchase in the financial markets. Therefore, the amount of deposits that wage earners spend in the goods market and in the financial markets is a measure of all new deposits returning to firms. Firms use these deposits to repay banks for their initial loans. This is what has been labelled the Kaldor–Trevithick reflux mechanism (Kaldor and Trevithick 1981). Horizontalists use this mechanism in order to explain how 'excess' deposits for wage earners are extinguished from the money supply process (Lavoie 1999: 105–108).

Structuralists usually acknowledge the importance of the Kaldor–Trevithick reflux mechanism (e.g. Arestis 1988: 65). However, they argue that the reflux mechanism does not automatically extinguish all newly created deposits (Chick 1986: 205, Cottrell 1986: 17, Dalziel 2001: 144(2), Palley 1991: 397). Wage earners spend part of these deposits in the goods market and save the remainder for precautionary or speculative purposes. The consequent allocation of deposits between securities and liquid balances is a portfolio choice, and for this reason it cannot be divorced from changes in interest rate differentials, which are bound to have important repercussions in the loans market (Arestis and Howells 1996: 540–544). Structuralists thus maintain that the portfolio choice of wage earners between securities and liquid balances is an important component of the money supply process. It demonstrates the relevance of feedback effects between the credit market and the financial markets.

Figure 8.3 shows the differences between the Horizontalist and Structuralist analyses of the financial markets.[6] The significant changes from

6 The author is indebted to Peter Howells for comments and suggestions on the graphical representation of the controversial issues surrounding the behaviour of economic agents in the financial markets (see also Howells 2007).

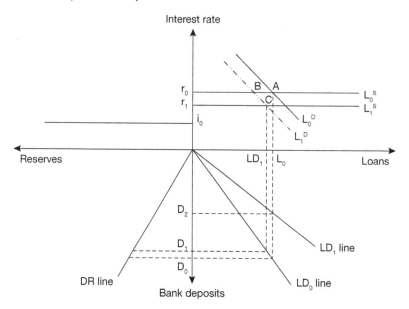

Figure 8.3 A general endogenous money analysis of the financial market

previous figures are the different slopes of the *LD* line, and the effects of this difference on the credit market. Again, for the sake of simplicity, the supply of reserves (R^S) is assumed to be perfectly elastic, meaning that only a single monetary policy is considered. As in the previous figures, the demand for loans (L_0^D) together with the supply of loans (L_0^S) determines the flow of new loans (L_0), and via the LD_0 line the flow of new deposits (D_0). Importantly, the LD_0 line is drawn for a given portfolio choice of wage earners between securities and liquid balances. Therefore, it cannot be excluded that the flow of new loans (L_0) creates an expansion of new deposits (D_0) which exceeds the willingness of wage earners to hold them. Wage earners will then modify their portfolios, attempting to hold fewer deposits (e.g. D_2) by exchanging some of the new deposits (D_0) for securities. The prices of securities will rise and yields will fall. The LD_0 line rotates anti-clockwise (e.g. LD_1 line). This also means that firms are now able to recover on the financial markets a greater proportion of the initial flow of new deposits (D_0), which in turn reduces their outstanding debts to the banks. The demand for new loans will thus shift inwards (e.g. L_1^D). At the same time, the fall in the yields on securities means that wage earners are now willing to hold a greater proportion of new deposits (e.g. D_1 rather than D_2). Similarly, it is likely that the fall in the yields on securities will also have an effect on the supply of new loans. Banks will lower their base rate (e.g. r_1), and the supply of new loans shifts downwards (e.g. L_I^S). To prevent cluttering Figure 8.3, the effects of these changes in the market for reserves are not explored here. In other words, a perfectly elastic schedule for the supply of reserves is assumed.

In short, Horizontalists have examined the two-way relationship between the credit market and the financial markets on the assumption that the ultimate impact of an expansion in the supply of loans has no effect whatsoever on the portfolios of wage earners. Structuralists have considered the possibility of portfolio choices changing as a result of the supply of new deposits. How portfolio adjustments in the financial markets affect future conditions in the credit market is of the utmost importance in their understanding of the money supply process (Arestis and Howells 1999: 118, also Cottrell 1988: 296, Goodhart 1989b: 32–33, Wolfson 1996: 458–461).

A single period-continuation interpretation of the controversial issues

The foregoing account of the markets for reserves, credit and financial instruments suggests that Horizontalists and Structuralists have in mind two distinct classes of models of the money supply process. These models share the same methodological and theoretical framework, but they differ in terms of the particular assumptions made about the state of expectations of central banks, banks, firms and wage earners. The purpose of the final section of this chapter is to give precise meaning to this idea. The Hicksian distinction between a single period and a continuation theory of money introduced in Chapter 6 is now used to explain the limits to the domains of relevance of the Horizontalist and Structuralist analyses of endogenous money (Fontana 2003b). This argument is offered in a reconciliatory spirit. In harmony with the encompassing principle discussed in Chapter 2, the final objective of this chapter is to encompass these analyses within a more general theory of endogenous money.[7]

Horizontalists and Structuralists concur that the general aim of endogenous money theory is to explain the process of creation and circulation of money. They recognise that calendar time normally elapses between the moment in which central bankers, banks, firms and wage earners make decisions and the ultimate outcome of these decisions. During this time, disappointment or new opportunities play a central role in shaping and

---

7 For a through discussion of the encompassing principle as an appropriate characterisation of the Post Keynesian way of thinking, see Fontana and Gerrard (2002a). Recent examples of the encompassing principle in practice are Fontana and Palacio-Vera (2002, 2003).

constraining the behaviour of these agents. Accordingly, these agents continuously revise their plans and expectations for the future course of events.

Having acknowledged the relevance of calendar time and expectations, Horizontalist and Structuralist analyses seem to differ in terms of alternative assumptions about the state of expectations involved in the money supply process, and their influence on the working of the markets for monetary reserves, credit and financial instruments. From this perspective, Horizontalists and Structuralists have proposed what in the previous two chapters have been labelled a single period analysis of endogenous money and a continuation analysis of endogenous money, respectively (Hicks 1956: 223).

A single period is the minimum effective unit of economic time for the analysis of agents involved in the money supply process. The length of this period is such that changes in expectations never occur within it, but rather at the junction of one single period and the next. A single period theory of endogenous money is thus built on the simple assumption that the state of agents' expectations is given. It is given in the sense not of being exogenous, but rather of being assumed constant. This assumption allows the specification of simple and stable functional relationships that continuously changing expectations would have made difficult or impossible to study. It is a realistic attempt to specify the fundamental relationships of the money supply process, without ignoring the possibility that changes in the state of expectations may affect the behaviour of agents involved in this process.

Notwithstanding these positive features, the previous section has shown the limitations of a single period analysis of endogenous money. The possibility that central banks may adopt new monetary stances in response to conditions in the credit market, that over the business cycle banks may revise price and non-price terms of credit, or that the changes in the portfolios of wage earners may affect the lending activity of banks – all these possibilities have no place in a single period analysis. This should not come as a surprise. The formal features of a single period narrow the issues that can be investigated within such a time frame. In a single period, expectations can be frustrated, but their effects are not allowed to alter the current course of events. The effects of changes in the state of expectations have to wait for the next single period.

There are interesting lessons to be learnt when expectations are allowed to affect the course of events. The actual path followed by the sequence of activities that describes the money supply process is explained by the interactions between what agents actually planned to do and what, they discover, they should have planned to do. This is the primary purpose of the continuation analysis of money, which is concerned with the effects of the events of a period upon the expectations that determine the events of the following periods. A continuation analysis is thus the natural complement to a single period analysis. It is the analysis of a dynamic sequence of single periods. It deals explicitly with linkages between successive periods, and these linkages are an essential step in moving beyond the boundaries of self-contained single periods.

The time framework of a continuation analysis explicitly allows for the fact that the general state of expectations may change in the light of realised results. Inconsistencies between the plans of agents come to the forefront in this analysis as all sorts of mechanisms work to reconcile them. For example, if a central bank were to realise that the actual outcome of its monetary policy was less favourable than it had expected, it would take action to prevent the situation from deteriorating further. As its expectations interact with the realised level of demand for monetary reserves, the short-run nominal interest rate would be likely to change to reflect the new conditions in the economy. The base interest rates would then be affected, as would the demand for loans and the holding of deposits. Thus, the new aggregate supply of reserves would be responding to conditions in the credit market, and the financial markets. Policy reactions from the reserve markets would finally feed back to these markets, creating a complex network of interactions between all the agents involved in the money supply process.

These interactions, policy reactions and feedback mechanisms are important features of continuation analysis, and they constitute a major difference from single period analysis. Staying with the same example, the latter would show that demand and supply conditions in the reserve market affect the credit market. A single period would then continue for a sufficient length of time such that the loans supply process works itself out completely. During this period, a central bank may be disappointed by the results of its policy, commercial banks may experience new opportunities and unexpected problems, or wage earners may prefer to change their portfolios. Yet, the formal features of the single period imply that disappointments, new opportunities or preferences would not have any effect on the state of expectations, and hence on the behaviour of agents operating in the reserve, credit and financial markets. It is only in the next period that these markets would record new demand and supply conditions.

Before concluding, a word of caution is required. As argued in Chapter 6, the Hicksian distinction between a single period analysis and a continuation analysis does not imply that the former is necessarily less important or relevant than the latter. The advantage of the Hicksian distinction is that there is a rigorous criterion to discriminate between these two types of analysis which differ in the assumptions about the state of expectations of agents. Which type of analysis is more important or relevant depends on the purpose of the analysis, and which assumption about the state of expectations of agents is more realistic in the situation analysed. For instance, Figure 8.1 represents the supply of reserves as a step function, with each horizontal segment indicating a different interest rate policy. The reason for a step function is that in a continuation analysis of the reserve market, the central bank has the possibility of responding to conditions in the credit market, and hence of changing their monetary policy stance (e.g. i_0, i_1). However, this does not mean that the single period representation of the supply of reserves as a horizontal line has little relevance in the analysis of the reserve market. The case could indeed be made that in normal circumstances the latter is the most appropriate representation of the supply of reserves. The actions of the central bank in the reserve market are normally defensive, i.e. it intervenes in order to achieve rather than to change the monetary policy stance. This means that in reasonably stable economic and financial conditions it is more appropriate to assume that the state of expectations of the central bank is broadly constant. By the same token, in unstable economic and financial conditions which give rise to changing expectations, a continuation analysis of the market for reserves is likely to be more relevant. In other words, in unstable conditions it is important to rely on a time frame model that allows for all sorts of dynamic reactions between the reserve, credit and financial markets.

Conclusions

The core of endogenous money theory is that the supply of money in modern economies is determined by the demand for loans, and that this in turn responds to the need for financing production, accumulation, consumer durable goods or speculative purchases. Beyond a widespread agreement over the idea that 'loans create deposits' and 'deposits generate reserves', there is much controversy. Horizontalists and Structuralists have now debated for a long time the key issues related to endogenous money. Do central banks accommodate the demand for reserves at the going short-run nominal interest rate? Does the supply of loans slope upwards? Do wage earners make portfolio choices that affect the future availability of credit?

This chapter has built on the analysis of the main features of the Horizontalist and Structuralist analyses of endogenous money discussed in Chapter 7. It has thus proposed an original four-panel diagram to review the areas of controversy between Horizontalist and Structuralist analyses of endogenous money, before showing that there is a more general framework in which these analyses can be made compatible. This general theory of endogenous money is based on Hicks's distinction between single period and continuation analysis, and it can used to analyse specific institutional settings or specific historical instances. From this perspective, the current disagreements between Horizontalists and Structuralists arise from the particular assumptions made about the general state of expectations of economic agents. Horizontalists rely upon a single period analysis that is built on the assumption that the state of expectations of all agents involved in the money supply process is constant. This assumption allows the specification of stable functional relationships that continuously changing expectations would make very laborious to specify. On the other hand, Structuralists depend on a continuation framework that explicitly takes account of the fact that the state of expectations of agents may change in the light of realised results. In this way, Structuralists are able to tackle controversial issues related to shifting monetary policies, the liquidity preference of banks and the loans–deposits nexus that are overlooked by Horizontalists. The conclusion of this chapter is that the Horizontalist and Structuralist analyses together form a more general theory of endogenous money.

Bibliography

Akerlof, G.A. (2002) 'Behavioral macroeconomics and macroeconomic behavior', *American Economic Review*, 92(3): 411–433.

Ambrosi, G.M. (2004) *Keynes, Pigou, Cambridge Keynesians: authenticity and analytical perspective in the Keynes-Classics debate*, Basingstoke: Palgrave Macmillan.

Arestis, P. (1988) 'Post Keynesian theory of money, credit and finance', in P. Arestis (ed.) (1988) *Post-Keynesian Monetary Economics: new approaches to financial modelling*, Aldershot: Edward Elgar.

—— (1992) *The Post-Keynesian Approach to Economics*, Aldershot: Edward Elgar.

—— (1996) 'Post-Keynesian economics: towards coherence', *Cambridge Journal of Economics*, 20(1): 111–135.

Arestis P. and Howells P. (1996) 'Theoretical reflection on endogenous money: the problem with convenience lending', *Cambridge Journal of Economics*, 20(5): 539–552.

—— (1999) 'The supply of credit money and the demand for deposits: a reply', *Cambridge Journal of Economics*, 23(1): 115–119.

Arestis, P. and Sawyer, M.C. (eds) (2006) *A Handbook of Alternative Monetary Economics*, Cheltenham: Edward Elgar.

Arestis, P., Dunn, S.P. and Sawyer, M.C. (1999) 'On the coherence of Post-Keynesian economics: a comment on Walters and Young', *Scottish Journal of Political Economy*, 46(3): 339–345.

Backhouse, R.E. (1998) 'The value of Post Keynesian economics: a neoclassical response to Harcourt and Hamouda', in R.E. Backhouse (ed.) (1998) *Explorations in Economic Methodology*, London: Routledge.

Bell, S. (2003) 'Liquidity preference', in J.E. King (ed.) (2003) *The Elgar Companion to Post Keynesian Economics*, Cheltenham: Edward Elgar.

Bellofiore, R. (1994) 'Poverty of rhetoric: Keynes versus McCloskey', in A. Marzola and F. Silva (eds) (1994) *John Maynard Keynes: language and method*, Aldershot: Edward Elgar.

Bellofiore, R. and Ferri, P. (eds) (2001) *The Economic Legacy of Hyman Minsky*, Cheltenham: Edward Elgar.

Bertocco, G. (2001) 'Is Kaldor's theory of money supply endogeneity still relevant?', *Metroeconomica*, 52(1): 95–120.

Bibow, J. (1998) 'On Keynesian theories of liquidity preference', *The Manchester School*, 66(2): 238–273.

—— (2006) 'Liquidity preference theory', in P. Arestis and M.C. Sawyer (eds) (2006) *A Handbook of Alternative Monetary Economics*, Cheltenham: Edward Elgar.

Binmore, K. (1999) 'Why experiment in economics?' *Economic Journal*, 109(453): F16–F24.

Bliss, C.J. (1975) *Capital Theory and the Distribution of Income*, Amsterdam: Elsevier North-Holland.

Braithwaite, R.B. (1973) 'Editorial foreword', in *The Collected Writings of J.M. Keynes* (1973), vol. VIII, London: Macmillan for the Royal Economic Society.

Brown, A., Slater, G. and Spencer, D.A. (2002) 'Driven to abstraction? Critical realism and the search for the 'inner connection' of social phenomena', *Cambridge Journal of Economics*, 26(6): 773–788.

Brunner, K. (1986) 'Keynes's intellectual legacy,' in J. Burton *et al.* (eds) (1986) *Keynes's General Theory: fifty years on*, London: Institute of Economic Affairs.

Carabelli, A.M. (1985) 'Cause, chance and possibility', in T. Lawson and H. Pesaran (eds) (1985) *Keynes's Economics: methodological issues*, London: Croom Helm.

—— (1988) *On Keynes's Method*, London: Macmillan.

—— (1991) 'The methodology of the critique of classical theory: Keynes on organic interdependence,' in B.W. Bateman and J.B. Davis (eds) (1991) *Keynes and Philosophy: essays on the origin of Keynes's thought*, Aldershot: Edward Elgar.

Carvalho, F.J. (1988) 'Keynes on probability, uncertainty and decision making', *Journal of Post Keynesian Economics*, 11(1): 66–81.

—— (1992) *Keynes and the Post Keynesians*, Aldershot: Edward Elgar.

Chick, V. (1983) *Macroeconomics After Keynes: a reconsideration of the* General Theory, Oxford: Philip Allan and Cambridge, MA: MIT Press.

—— (1986) 'The evolution of the banking system and the theory of saving, investment and interest rate', *Économies et Sociétés*, 20(8–9): 111–126; reprinted in P. Arestis and S.C. Dow (eds) (1992) *On Money, Method, and Keynes: selected essays by Victoria Chick*, London: Macmillan; and also in M. Musella and C. Panico (eds) (1995) *The Money Supply in the Economic Process: a Post Keynesian perspective*, Aldershot: Edward Elgar.

—— (1992) *On Money, Method and Keynes: selected essays by Victoria Chick*, London: Macmillan.

—— (1995a) 'Is there a case for Post Keynesian economics?', *Scottish Journal of Political Economy*, 42(1): 20–36.

—— (1995b) '"Order out of chaos" in economics', in S. Dow and J. Hillard (eds) (1995) *Keynes, Knowledge, and Uncertainty*, Aldershot: Edward Elgar.

Chick, V. and Caserta, M. (1997) 'Provisional equilibrium and macroeconomic theory', in P. Arestis, G. Palma and M.C. Sawyer (eds) (1997) *Markets,*

Unemployment and Economic Policy: essays in honour of Geoff Harcourt, vol. II, London: Routledge.

Chick, V. and Dow, S.C. (2001) 'Formalism, logic and reality: a Keynesian analysis', *Cambridge Journal of Economics*, 25(6): 705–721.

Clower, R. and Leijonhufvud, A. (1975) 'The coordination of economic activities: a Keynesian perspective', *American Economic Review*, 65(2): 182–188.

Coddington, A. (1976) 'Keynesian economics: the search for first principles', *Journal of Economic Literature*, 14(7): 1258–1273.

Cohen, A.J. and Harcourt, G.C. (2003) 'Whatever happened to the Cambridge capital theory controversies?', *Journal of Economic Perspectives*, 17(1): 199–214.

Collard, D.A. (1984) 'The ascent of high theory: a view from the foothills', in D.A. Collard *et al.* (eds) (1984) *Economic Theory and Hicksian Themes*, Oxford: Oxford University Press.

—— (1993) 'High Hicks, deep Hicks, and equilibrium', *History of Political Economy*, 25(2): 331–350.

Collard D.A., Helm D.R., Scott M.F.G., and Sen, A.K. (eds) (1984) *Economic Theory and Hicksian Themes*, Oxford: Oxford University Press.

Cottrell, A. (1986) 'The endogeneity of money and money-income causality', *Scottish Journal of Political Economy*, 33(1): 2–27.

—— (1988) 'The endogeneity of money: reply', *Scottish Journal of Political Economy*, 35(3): 295–297.

—— (1994) 'Post-Keynesian monetary economics', *Cambridge Journal of Economics*, 18(6): 587–605.

Critical Realism (1999) *Journal of Post Keynesian Economics*, Special Issue, Fall, 22(1): 3–129.

—— (2002) *Cambridge Journal of Economics*, Special Issue, 26(6): 679–821.

Crotty, J.R. (1980) 'Post-Keynesian economic theory: an overview and evaluation', *American Economic Review*, Papers and Proceedings, 70(2): 20–25.

Currie, M. and Steedman, I. (1990) *Wrestling with Time*, Manchester: Manchester University Press.

Dalziel, P. (1996) 'The Keynesian multiplier, liquidity preference, and endogenous money', *Journal of Post Keynesian Economics*, 18(3): 311–331.

—— (2000) 'A Post Keynesian theory of asset price inflation with endogenous money', *Journal of Post Keynesian Economics*, 22(2): 227–245.

—— (2001) *Money, Credit and Price Stability*, London: Routledge.

Darity, W. Jr and Young, W. (1995) '*IS-LM*: an inquest', *History of Political Economy*, 27(1): 1–41.

Davidson, P. (1965) 'Keynes' finance motive', *Oxford Economic Papers*, 17(1): 47–65.

—— (1972) *Money and the Real World*, London: Macmillan.

—— (1982–83) 'Rational expectations: a fallacious foundation for studying crucial decision-making processes', *Journal of Post Keynesian Economics*, 5(2): 182–196.

—— (1994) *Post Keynesian Macroeconomic Theory*, Cheltenham: Edward Elgar.

—— (1996) 'Reality and economic theory', *Journal of Post Keynesian Economics*, 18(4): 479–508.

—— (2003) 'Setting the record straight on *A History of Post Keynesian Economics*', *Journal of Post Keynesian Economics*, 26(2): 245–272.

—— (2007) *John Maynard Keynes*, Basingstoke: Palgrave Macmillan

Davidson, P. and Smolensky, E. (1964) *Aggregate Supply and Demand Analysis*, New York: Harper and Row.

Deleplace, G. and Nell, E.J. (eds) (1996) *Money in Motion*, London: Macmillan.

Dequech, D. (1997) 'Uncertainty in a strong sense: meaning and sources', *Economic Issues*, 2(2): 21–43.

De Vroey, M. (1999) 'J.R. Hicks on equilibrium and disequilibrium: *Value and Capital* revisited', *History of Economics Review*, 29(Winter): 35–44.

Dixon, H.D. (2000) 'New-Keynesian macroeconomics: the role of theory and evidence', in R.E. Backhouse and A. Salanti (eds) (2000) *Macroeconomics and the Real World*, vol. 2, Oxford: Oxford University Press.

Dobb, M. (1937) 'The trend of modern economics', in *Political Economy and Capitalism*, London: Routledge and Kegan Paul; reprinted in E.K. Hunt and J.G. Schwartz (eds) (1972) *A Critique of Economic Theory: selected readings*, Harmondsworth: Penguin Books.

Docherty, P. (2005) *Money and Employment: a study of the theoretical implications of endogenous money*, Cheltenham: Edward Elgar.

Dostaler, G. (2007) *Keynes and his Battles*, Cheltenham: Edward Elgar.

Dow, S.C. (1984) 'Methodology and the analysis of a monetary economy', *Économies et Sociétés, Monnaie et Production*, 18(1): 7–35; reprinted in *Money and the Economic Process* (1993), Aldershot: Edward Elgar.

—— (1992) 'Post-Keynesian methodology: a comment', *Review of Political Economy*, 4(1): 111–113.

—— (1995a) 'Interview', in J. King (ed.) (1995) *Conversations with Post Keynesians*, London: Macmillan.

—— (1995b) 'The appeal of neoclassical economics: some insights from Keynes's epistemology', *Cambridge Journal of Economics*, 19(6): 715–733.

—— (1995c) 'Uncertainty about uncertainty', in S.C. Dow and J. Hillard (eds) (1995) *Keynes, Knowledge, and Uncertainty*, Aldershot: Edward Elgar.

—— (1996a) 'Horizontalism: a critique', *Cambridge Journal of Economics*, 20(4): 497–508.

—— (1996b) 'Keynes's philosophy and post Keynesian monetary theory', in P. Arestis (ed.) (1996) *Keynes, Money and the Open Economy: essays in honour of Paul Davidson*, Cheltenham: Edward Elgar.

—— (1996c) *The Methodology of Macroeconomic Thought: a conceptual analysis of schools of thought in economics*, Cheltenham: Edward Elgar.

—— (1997) 'Endogenous money', in G.C. Harcourt and P.A. Riach (eds) (1997) *A 'Second Edition' of the* General Theory, London: Routledge.

—— (1998) 'Formalism in economics', *Economic Journal*, 108(451): 1826–1828.

—— (1999) 'Post Keynesianism and Critical Realism: what is the connection?', *Journal of Post Keynesian Economics*, 22(1): 15–33.

—— (2002) *Economic Methodology: an inquiry*, Oxford: Oxford University Press.

—— (2006) 'Endogenous money: structuralist', in P. Arestis and M.C. Sawyer (eds) (2006) *A Handbook of Alternative Monetary Economics*, Cheltenham: Edward Elgar.

Dow, A.C. and Dow, S.C. (1989) 'Endogenous money creation and idle balances', in J. Pheby (ed.) (1989) *New Directions in Post Keynesian Economics*, Aldershot: Edward Elgar; reprinted in M. Musella and C. Panico (eds) (1995) *The Money Supply in the Economic Process: a Post Keynesian perspective*, Aldershot: Edward Elgar.

Dow, S.C. and Hillard, J. (1995) *Keynes, Knowledge, and Uncertainty*, Aldershot: Edward Elgar.

Dow, S.C. and Rodríguez-Fuentes, C. (1998) 'The political economy of monetary policy', in P. Arestis and M.C. Sawyer (eds) (1998) *The Political Economy of Central Banking*, Cheltenham: Edward Elgar.

Dow, S.C. and Smithin, J. (1999) 'The structure of financial markets and the "first principles" of monetary economics', *Scottish Journal of Political Economy*, 46(1): 72–90.

Downward, P.M. and Mearman A. (2002) 'Critical realism and econometrics: constructive dialogue with Post Keynesian economics', *Metroeconomica*, 53(4): 391–415.

Downward, P.M., Finch, J.H. and Ramsay, J. (2002) 'Critical realism, empirical methods and inference: a critical discussion', *Cambridge Journal of Economics*, 26(4): 481–500.

Eatwell, J. (1979) 'Theories of value, output and employment', *Thames Papers in Political Economy*, London: Thames Polytechnic; reprinted in J. Eatwell and M. Milgate (eds) (1983) *Keynes's Economics and the Theory of Value and Distribution*, London: Duckworth.

—— (1987) 'Keynesianism', in J. Eatwell, M. Milgate and P. Newman (eds) (1987) *The New Palgrave: a dictionary of economics*, vol. 3, London: Palgrave Macmillan.

Economist (2007) 'The great northern run', 384(8547): 96.

Eichner, A.S. (1973) 'A theory of the determination of the mark-up under oligopoly', *Economic Journal*, 83(332): 1184–1200; reprinted in M.C. Sawyer (ed.) (1988) *Post-Keynesian Economics*, Aldershot: Edward Elgar.

—— (1976) *The Megacorp and Oligopoly: micro foundations of macro dynamics*, Cambridge: Cambridge University Press.

—— (1979) 'Introduction', in A.S. Eichner (ed.) (1979) *A Guide to Post-Keynesian Economics*, London: Macmillan.

Eichner, A.S. and Kregel, J. (1975) 'An essay on Post-Keynesian theory: a new paradigm in economics', *Journal of Economic Literature*, 13(4): 1293–1314; reprinted in M.C. Sawyer (ed.) (1988) *Post-Keynesian Economics*, Aldershot: Edward Elgar.

Fitzgibbons, A. (1988) *Keynes's Vision: a new political economy*, Oxford: Clarendon Press.

Fontana, G. (1997) 'La théorie du crédit d'Emile Mireaux: "Les miracles du crédit"', *Revue d'Économie Politique*, 107(2): 285–294.

—— (2000) 'Post Keynesians and Circuitists on money and uncertainty: an attempt at generality', *Journal of Post Keynesian Economics*, 23(1): 27–48.

—— (2003a) 'Keynes's *A Treatise on Money*', in J. King (ed.) (2003) *Elgar Companion to Post Keynesian Economics*, Cheltenham: Edward Elgar.

—— (2003b) 'Post Keynesian approaches to endogenous money: a time framework explanation', *Review of Political Economy*, 15(3): 291–314.

—— (2004) 'Hicks on monetary theory and history: money as endogenous money', *Cambridge Journal of Economics*, 28(1): 73–88.

—— (2006) 'Telling better stories in macroeconomic textbooks: monetary policy, endogenous money and aggregate demand', in M. Setterfield (ed.) (2006) *Complexity, Endogenous Money and Macroeconomic Theory: essays in honour of Basil Moore*, Cheltenham: Edward Elgar.

—— (2007) 'Why money matters: Wicksell, Keynes and the "New Consensus View" on monetary policy', *Journal of Post Keynesian Economics*, 30(1): 43–60.

Fontana, G. and Gerrard, B. (1999) 'Disequilibrium states and adjustment processes: towards a historical-time analysis of behaviour under uncertainty', *Philosophical Psychology*, 12(3): 311–324.

—— (2002a) 'The encompassing principle as an emerging methodology for Post Keynesian economics', in P. Arestis, M. Desai and S.C. Dow (eds) (2002) *Methodology, Microeconomics and Keynes: essays in honour of Victoria Chick*, vol. 2, London: Routledge.

—— (2002b) 'The monetary context of economic behaviour', *Review of Social Economy*, 60(2): 243–262.

—— (2004) 'A Post Keynesian theory of decision-making under uncertainty', *Journal of Economic Psychology*, 25(5): 619–637.

—— (2006) 'The future of Post Keynesian economics', *Banca Nazionale del Lavoro Quarterly Review*, 59(236): 49–80.

Fontana, G. and Palacio-Vera, A. (2002) 'Monetary policy rules: what are we learning?', *Journal of Post Keynesian Economics*, 24(4): 547–568.

—— (2003) 'Modern theory and practice of central banking: an endogenous money perspective', in L.P. Rochon and S. Rossi (eds) (2003) *Modern Theories of Money: the nature and role of money in capitalist economies*, Cheltenham: Edward Elgar.

—— (2004) 'Monetary policy uncovered: theory and practice', *International Review of Applied Economics*, 18(1): 25–42.

Fontana, G. and Realfonzo, R. (eds) (2005) *The Monetary Theory of Production: tradition and perspectives*, London: Palgrave Macmillan.

Garegnani, P. (1978) 'Notes on consumption, investment and effective demand: part I', *Cambridge Journal of Economics*, 2(4): 335–353.

—— (1979) 'Notes on consumption, investment and effective demand: part II', *Cambridge Journal of Economics*, 3(1): 63–82.

Gerrard, B. (1989) *Theory of a Capitalist Economy: towards a Post-Classical synthesis*, Oxford: Basil Blackwell.

—— (1991) 'Keynes's *General Theory*: interpreting the interpretations', *Economic Journal*, 101(405): 276–287.

—— (1992a) 'Human logic in Keynes's thought: escape from the Cartesian vice', in P. Arestis and V. Chick (eds) (1992) *Recent Development in Post-Keynesian Economics*, Aldershot: Edward Elgar.

—— (1992b) 'From *A Treatise on Probability* to the *General Theory*: continuity or change in Keynes's thought?', in B. Gerrard and J. Hillard (eds) (1992) *The Philosophy and Economics of J.M. Keynes*, Aldershot: Edward Elgar.

—— (1995) 'Keynes, the Keynesians and the Classics: a suggested interpretation', *Economic Journal*, 105(429): 445–458.

—— (1997) 'Method and methodology in Keynes's *General Theory*', in G.C. Harcourt and P.A. Riach (eds) (1997) *A 'Second Edition' of the* General Theory, vol. 2, London: Routledge.

—— (2003) 'Fundamentalist Keynesianism', in J. King (ed.) (2003) *The Elgar Companion to Post Keynesian Economics*, Cheltenham: Edward Elgar.

Godley, W. and Lavoie M. (2007) *Monetary Economics: an integrated approach to credit, money, income, production and wealth*, London: Palgrave Macmillan.

Goodhart, C.A.E. (1989a) *Money, Information and Uncertainty*, 2nd edn, London: Macmillan.

—— (1989b) 'Has Moore become too horizontal?', *Journal of Post Keynesian Economics*, 12(1): 29–34; reprinted in M. Musella and C. Panico (eds) (1995) *The Money Supply in the Economic Process: a Post Keynesian perspective*, Aldershot: Edward Elgar.

—— (2002) 'The endogeneity of money', in P. Arestis, M. Desai and S.C. Dow (eds) (2002) *Money, Macroeconomics and Keynes: essays in honour of Victoria Chick*, London: Routledge.

Graziani, A. (1984) 'The debate on Keynes' finance motive', *Economic Notes*, 13(1): 5–32.

—— (1989) 'The theory of the monetary circuit', *Thames Papers in Political Economy*, London: Thames Polytechnic; reprinted in M. Musella and C. Panico (eds) (1995) *The Money Supply in the Economic Process: a Post Keynesian perspective*, Aldershot: Edward Elgar

—— (1991) 'La théorie keynésienne de la monnaie et le financement de l'économie', *Économie Appliquée*, 44(1): 25–41.

—— (1996) 'Money as purchasing power and money as a stock of wealth in Keynesian economic thought', in G. Deleplace and E.J. Nell (eds) (1996) *Money in Motion*, London: Macmillan.

—— (2003) *The Monetary Theory of Production*, Cambridge: Cambridge University Press.

Greenwald, B. and Stiglitz, J.E. (1987) 'Keynesian, New Keynesian and New Classical Economics', *Oxford Economic Papers*, 39(1): 119–132.

Hagemann, H. and Hamouda, O.F. (1994) 'Introduction', in H. Hagemann and O.F. Hamouda (eds) (1994) *The Legacy of Hicks: his contributions to economic analysis*, London: Routledge.

Hahn, F.H. (1973a) 'The winter of our discontent', *Economica*, 40(159): 322–330; reprinted in *Equilibrium and Macroeconomics* (1984), Oxford: Basil Blackwell.

—— (1973b) 'On the foundations of monetary theory', in M. Parkin and A.R. Nobay (eds) (1973) *Essays in Modern Economics*, London: Longman; reprinted in *Equilibrium and Macroeconomics* (1984), Oxford: Basil Blackwell.

—— (1994) 'John Hicks the theorist', in H. Hagemann and O.F. Hamouda (eds)

(1994) *The Legacy of Hicks: his contributions to economic analysis*, London: Routledge.

Hammond, P.J. (1987) 'Uncertainty', in J. Eatwell, M. Milgate and P. Newman (eds) (1987) *The New Palgrave: a dictionary of economics*, vol. 4, London: Palgrave Macmillan.

Hamouda, O.F. and Harcourt, G.C. (1989) 'Post-Keynesianism: from criticism to coherence?', *Bulletin of Economic Research*, 40(1): 1–33; reprinted in J. Pheby (ed.) (1989) *New Directions in Post-Keynesian Economics*, Aldershot: Edward Elgar.

Hamouda, O.F. and Smithin, J.N. (1988) 'Some remarks on "Uncertainty and Economic Analysis"', *Economic Journal*, 98(389): 159–164.

Hansson, B.A. (1982) *The Stockholm School and the Development of Dynamic Method*, London: Croom Helm.

Harcourt, G.C. (1972) *Some Cambridge Controversies in the Theory of Capital*, Cambridge: Cambridge University Press.

—— (1975) 'Revival of political economy: a further comment', *Economic Record*, 51(3): 368–371.

—— (1992) 'The legacy of Keynes: theoretical methods and unfinished business', in C. Sardoni (ed.) (1992) *On Political Economists and Modern Political Economy: selected essays of G.C. Harcourt*, London: Routledge.

—— (1998) 'The Cambridge contribution to economics', in S.J. Ormrod (ed.) *Cambridge Contributions*, Cambridge: Cambridge University Press; reprinted in *50 Years a Keynesian and Other Essays* (2001), Basingstoke: Palgrave Macmillan.

—— (1999) 'Post-Keynesian thought', unpublished; printed in *50 Years a Keynesian and Other Essays* (2001), Basingstoke: Palgrave Macmillan.

—— (2004) 'The economics of Keynes and its theoretical and political importance: or, what would Marx and Keynes have made of the happenings of the past 30 years and more?', *Post-autistic Economics Review*, 27(9): article 1, www.paecon.net/PAEReview/issue27/Harcourt27.htm

—— (2006) *The Structure of Post-Keynesian Economics: the core contributions of the pioneers*, Cambridge: Cambridge University Press.

Harcourt, G.C. and Kenyon, P. (1976) 'Pricing and the investment decision', *Kyklos*, 29(3): 449–477; reprinted in M.C. Sawyer (ed.) (1988) *Post-Keynesian Economics*, Aldershot: Edward Elgar.

Harrod, R.F. (1937) 'Mr Keynes and traditional theory', *Econometrica*, 5(1): 74–86.

—— (1939) 'An essay in dynamic theory', *Economic Journal*, 49(193): 14–33.

—— (1948) *Towards a Dynamic Economics*, London: Macmillan.

—— (1951) *The Life of John Maynard Keynes*, London: Macmillan.

Hayes, M.G. (2006) *The Economics of Keynes: a new guide to the* General Theory, Cheltenham: Edward Elgar.

Hein, E. (2008) *Money, Distribution Conflict and Capital Accummulation*, Basingstoke: Palgrave Macmillan.

Hewitson, G. (1995) 'Post-Keynesian monetary theory: some issues', *Journal of Economic Surveys*, 9(3): 285–310.

Hicks, J.R. (1933) 'Gleichgewicht und Knojunktur', *Zeitschrift für Nationalökonomie*, 4: 441–455; translated as 'Equilibrium and the cycle', *Economic Inquiry*, 1980, 18(4): 523–534; reprinted in *Money, Interest and Wages: collected essays on economic theory* (1982), vol. 2, Oxford: Basil Blackwell.

—— (1935) 'A suggestion for simplifying the theory of money', *Economica*, New Series, 2(5): 1–19; reprinted in *Critical Essays in Monetary Theory* (1967), Oxford: Clarendon Press; and also with addendum in *Money, Interest and Wages: collected essays on economic theory* (1982), vol. 2, Oxford: Basil Blackwell.

—— (1937) 'Mr Keynes and the "Classics"', *Econometrica*, 5(2): 147–159; reprinted in *Critical Essays in Monetary Theory* (1967), Oxford: Clarendon Press; and also with addendum in *Money, Interest and Wages: collected essays on economic theory* (1982), vol. 2, Oxford: Basil Blackwell.

—— (1939) *Value and Capital*, Oxford: Clarendon Press.

—— (1956) 'Methods of dynamic analysis', *Twenty-five Economic Essays in English, German and Scandinavian Languages in Honour of Erik Lindahl*, Stockholm: Ekonomisk Tidschrift; reprinted with addendum in *Money, Interest and Wages: collected essays on economic theory* (1982), vol. 2, Oxford: Basil Blackwell.

—— (1965) *Capital and Growth*, Oxford: Clarendon Press.

—— (1967a) 'Monetary theory and history: an attempt at perspective', in *Critical Essays in Monetary Theory* (1967), Oxford: Clarendon Press.

—— (1967b) 'Thornton's *Paper Credit* (1802)', in *Critical Essays in Monetary Theory* (1967), Oxford: Clarendon Press.

—— (1973) 'Recollections and documents', *Economica*, 40(157): 2–11; reprinted in *Economic Perspectives: further essays on money and growth* (1977), Oxford: Clarendon Press.

—— (1974) *The Crisis in Keynesian Economics*, Oxford: Basil Blackwell.

—— (1975) 'Revival of political economy: the old and the new' (a reply to Harcourt), *Economic Record*, 51(3): 365–367.

—— (1976) 'Some questions of time in economics', in A.M. Tang, F.M. Westfield and J.S. Worley (eds) *Evolution, Welfare and Time in Economics: essays in honour of Nicholas Georgescu-Roegen*, Lexington, MA: Heath, Lexington Books; reprinted with addendum in *Money, Interest and Wages: collected essays on economic theory* (1982), vol. 2, Oxford: Basil Blackwell.

—— (1979) *Causality in Economics*, Oxford: Clarendon Press.

—— (1980) '*IS-LM*: an explanation', *Journal of Post Keynesian Economics*, 3(2): 139–154; reprinted with addendum in *Money, Interest and Wages: collected essays on economic theory* (1982), vol. 2, Oxford: Basil Blackwell.

—— (1982) 'Preface', in *Money, Interest and Wages: collected essays on economic theory* (1982), vol. 2, Oxford: Basil Blackwell.

—— (1983) 'A discipline not a science', in *Classics and Moderns: collected essays on economic theory* (1983), vol. 3, Oxford: Basil Blackwell.

—— (1985) *Methods of Dynamics Economics*, new edn of the first part of *Capital and Growth* (1965), Oxford: Clarendon Press.

—— (1989) *A Market Theory of Money*, Oxford: Clarendon Press.

—— (1991) 'The Swedish influence on *Value and Capital*', in L. Jonung (ed.) (1991) *The Stockholm School of Economics Revisited*, Cambridge: Cambridge University Press.

Hodgson, G. (1989) 'Post-Keynesianism and Institutionalism: the missing link', in J. Pheby (ed.) (1989) *New Directions in Post-Keynesian Economics*, Aldershot: Edward Elgar.

Howells, P.G.A. (1995) 'Endogenous money', *International Papers in Political Economy*, 2(2).

—— (2007) 'On some slippery slopes: horizontalists, structuralists and diagrams', University of the West of England: Mimeo.

Howitt, P. (1997) 'Expectations and uncertainty in contemporary Keynesian models', in G.C. Harcourt and P.A. Riach (eds) (1997) *A 'Second Edition' of the General Theory*, London: Routledge.

Ingham, G. (2004) *The Nature of Money*, Cambridge: Polity Press.

Kaldor, N. (1939) 'Speculation and economic stability', *Review of Economic Studies*, 7(1): 1–27.

—— (1940) 'A model of the trade cycle', *Economic Journal*, 50(197):78–92.

—— (1956) 'Alternative theories of distribution', *Review of Economic Studies*, 23(2): 83–100.

—— (1957) 'A model of economic growth', *Economic Journal*, 67(268): 591–624.

—— (1966) *Causes of the Slow Rate of Economic Growth of the United Kingdom: an inaugural lecture*, Cambridge: Cambridge University Press.

—— (1970a) 'The case for regional policies', *Scottish Journal of Political Economy*, 17(3): 337–348.

—— (1970b) 'The new Monetarism', *Lloyds Bank Review*, 97(1): 1–17.

—— (1982a) 'Keynes as an economic adviser', in A.P. Thirlwall (ed.) (1982) *Keynes as Policy Adviser*, London: Macmillan.

—— (1982b) *The Scourge of Monetarism*, Oxford: Oxford University Press.

Kaldor, N. and Mirrlees J. (1962) 'A new model of economic growth', *Review of Economic Studies*, 29(3): 174–192.

Kaldor, N. and Trevithick, J. (1981) 'A Keynesian perspective on money', *Lloyds Bank Review*, 1981(139): 1–19; reprinted in M.C. Sawyer (ed.) (1988) *Post-Keynesian Economics*, Aldershot: Edward Elgar.

Kalecki, M. (1939) *Essays in the Theory of Economic Fluctuations*, London: Allen and Unwin.

—— (1954) *Theory of Economic Dynamics*, London: Allen and Unwin.

Keynes, J.M. (1907) 'The principles of probability', manuscript, Cambridge: Marshall Library.

—— (1921) *A Treatise on Probability*, London: Macmillan; reprinted in *The Collected Writings of J.M. Keynes* (1973), vol. VIII, London: Macmillan for the Royal Economic Society.

—— (1926) 'Francis Ysidro Edgeworth 1845–1926', *Economic Journal*, 36: 140–153; reprinted in *The Collected Writings of J.M. Keynes: essays in biography* (1972), vol. X: 251–266, London: Macmillan for the Royal Economic Society.

—— (1930) *A Treatise on Money*, London: Macmillan; reprinted in *The Collected Writings of J.M. Keynes* (1971), vols V–VI, London: Macmillan for the Royal Economic Society.

—— (1931) 'Ramsey as a philosopher', *The New Statesman and the Nation*, 3(October); reprinted in *The Collected Writings of J.M. Keynes: essays in biography* (1972), vol. X: 336–339, London: Macmillan for the Royal Economic Society.

—— (1933a) 'Der stand und die nächste zundkunft der konjuncturforschung: festschrift für Arthur Spiethoff', trans. (1973) 'A monetary theory of production'; reprinted in *The Collected Writings of J.M. Keynes, the General Theory and After: part I preparation* (1973), vol. XIII: 408–411, London: Macmillan for the Royal Economic Society.

—— (1933b) 'Alfred Marshall', in *Essays in Biography*; reprinted in *The Collected Writings of J.M. Keynes: essays in biography* (1972), vol. X: 161–231, London: Macmillan for the Royal Economic Society.

—— (1933c) 'Definitions and ideas relating to capital: the concept of accounting period', typed fragment, University of Cambridge; reprinted in *The Collected Writings of J.M. Keynes, The General Theory and After: a supplement* (1979), vol. XXIX: 73–76, London: Macmillan for the Royal Economic Society.

—— (1935a) 'Letter to George Bernard Shaw: 1st January 1935'; reprinted in *The Collected Writings of J.M. Keynes, the General Theory and After: part I preparation* (1973), vol. XIII: 492–493, London: Macmillan for the Royal Economic Society.

—— (1935b) 'Robert Malthus: centenary allocution', *Economic Journal*, June; reprinted in *The Collected Writings of J.M. Keynes: essays in biography* (1972), vol. X: 104–108, London: Macmillan for the Royal Economic Society.

—— (1936) *The General Theory of Employment, Interest and Money*, London: Macmillan; reprinted in *The Collected Writings of J. M. Keynes* (1973), vol. VII, London: Macmillan for the Royal Economic Society.

—— (1937) 'The general theory of employment', *Quarterly Journal of Economics*, 51: 209–223; reprinted in *The Collected Writings of J.M. Keynes, the General Theory and After: part II defence and development* (1973), vol. XIV: 109–123, London: Macmillan for the Royal Economic Society.

—— (1938a) 'Letter to R.F. Harrod: 4th July, 1938', in *The Collected Writings of J.M. Keynes, the General Theory and After: part II defence and development* (1973), vol. XIV: 295–297, London: Macmillan for the Royal Economic Society.

—— (1938b) 'Letter to R.F. Harrod: 16th July, 1938', in *The Collected Writings of J.M. Keynes, the General Theory and After: part II defence and development* (1973), vol. XIV: 299–301, London: Macmillan for the Royal Economic Society.

—— (1938c) 'Letter to Mr Tyler: 23rd August, 1938', in *The Collected Writings of J.M. Keynes, the General Theory and After: part II defence and development* (1973), vol. XIV: 285–289, London: Macmillan for the Royal Economic Society.

—— (1938d) 'Letter to Dr Tinbergen: 20th September, 1938', in *The Collected Writings of J.M. Keynes, the General Theory and After: part II defence and development* (1973), vol. XIV: 293–295, London: Macmillan for the Royal Economic Society.

—— (1939) 'Professor Tinbergen's method', *Economic Journal*, September; reprinted in *The Collected Writings of J.M. Keynes, the General Theory and After: part II defence and development* (1973), vol. XIV: 306–318, London: Macmillan for the Royal Economic Society.

—— (1972) 'My early beliefs', reprinted in *The Collected Writings of J.M. Keynes: essays in biography* (1972) vol. X: 433–450, London: Macmillan for the Royal Economic Society.

—— (1979) 'Towards the *General Theory*'; reprinted in *The Collected Writings of J.M. Keynes, the General Theory and After: a supplement* (1979), vol. XXIX: 35–160, London: Macmillan for the Royal Economic Society.

King, J. (1995) *Post Keynesian Economics: an annotated bibliography*, Aldershot: Edward Elgar.

—— (2002) *A History of Post Keynesian Economics Since 1936*, Cheltenham: Edward Elgar.

—— (ed.) (2003) *The Elgar Companion to Post Keynesian Economics*, Cheltenham: Edward Elgar.

Kohn, M. (1986) 'Monetary analysis, the equilibrium method, and Keynes's "General Theory"', *Journal of Political Economy*, 94(6): 1191–1224.

Kregel, J.A. (1973) *The Reconstruction of Political Economy: an introduction to Post Keynesian economics*, London: Macmillan.

—— (1976) 'Economic methodology in the face of uncertainty: the modeling methods of Keynes and the Post-Keynesians', *Economic Journal*, 86(342): 209–225; reprinted in M.C. Sawyer (ed.) (1988) *Post-Keynesian Economics*, Aldershot: Edward Elgar.

—— (1980) 'Markets and institutions as features of a capitalist production system', *Journal of Post Keynesian Economics*, 3(1): 32–48.

—— (1987a) 'Effective demand', *The New Palgrave: a dictionary of economics*, London: Macmillan.

—— (1987b) 'Rational spirits and the Post Keynesian macroeconomic theory of microeconomics', *De Economist*, 135(4): 520–532.

Laidler, D. (1990) 'Hicks and the Classics: a review essay', *Journal of Monetary Economics*, 25(3): 481–489.

—— (1997) 'Notes on the microfoundations of monetary economics', *Economic Journal*, 107(443): 1213–1223.

—— (1999) *Fabricating the Keynesian Revolution: studies of the inter-war literature on money, the cycle, and unemployment*, Cambridge: Cambridge University Press.

Lavoie, M. (1992) *Foundations of Post-Keynesian Economics*, Aldershot: Edward Elgar.

—— (1996) 'Horizontalism, structuralism, liquidity preference and the principle of increasing risk', *Scottish Journal of Political Economy*, 43(3): 275–300.

—— (1999) 'The credit-led supply of deposits and the demand for money: Kaldor's reflux mechanism as previously endorsed by Joan Robinson', *Cambridge Journal of Economics*, 23(1): 103–113.

—— (2003) 'A primer on endogenous credit-money', in L.P. Rochon and S. Rossi (eds) (2003) *Modern Theories of Money: the nature and role of money in capitalist economies*, Cheltenham: Edward Elgar.

—— (2006) 'Endogenous money: accommodationist', in P. Arestis and M.C. Sawyer (eds) (2006) *A Handbook of Alternative Monetary Economics*, Cheltenham: Edward Elgar.

Lawson, T. (1985) 'Uncertainty and economic analysis', *Economic Journal*, 95(380): 909–927; reprinted in M.C. Sawyer (ed.) (1988) *Post-Keynesian Economics*, Aldershot: Edward Elgar.

—— (1987) 'The relative/absolute nature of knowledge and economic analysis', *Economic Journal*, 97(388): 951–970.

—— (1988) 'Probability and uncertainty in economic analysis', *Journal of Post Keynesian Economics*, 11(1): 38–65.

—— (1994) 'The nature of Post Keynesianism and its links to other traditions: a realist perspective', *Journal of Post Keynesian Economics*, 16(4): 503–538.

—— (1997) *Economics and Reality*, London: Routledge.

—— (1999) 'Connections and distinctions: Post Keynesianism and Critical Realism', *Journal of Post Keynesian Economics*, 22(1): 3–14.

—— (2003a) *Reorienting Economics*, London: Routledge.

—— (2003b) *Reclaiming Reality*, London and New York: Routledge.

Lawson, T. and Pesaran, H. (eds) (1985) *Keynes' Economics*, London: Croom Helm.

Lee, F. (1995) 'The death of Post Keynesian economics?', *Post Keynesian Study Group Newsletter*, January, 1–2.

—— (2000) 'The organisational history of Post Keynesian economics in America: 1971–1995', *Journal of Post Keynesian Economics*, 23(1): 141–162.

Leijonhufvud, A. (1968) *On Keynesian Economics and the Economics of Keynes: a study in monetary theory*, London: Oxford University Press.

—— (1981) 'Monetary theory in Hicksian perspective', in A. Leijonhufvud (ed.) (1981) *Information and Coordination: essays in macroeconomic theory*, Oxford: Oxford University Press.

—— (1984) 'Hicks on time and money', in D.A. Collard *et al.* (eds) (1984) *Economic Theory and Hicksian Themes*, Oxford: Oxford University Press.

Lindahl, E. (1929) 'Prisbildningsproblemet från kapitalteoretisk synpunkt', trans. 'The place of capital in the theory of price'; reprinted in E. Lindahl (ed.) (1939) *Studies in the Theory of Money and Capital*, London: George Allen and Unwin.

—— (1934a) 'Letter to Mr Keynes – 7 November 1934'; reprinted in *The Collected Writings of J.M. Keynes, the* General Theory *and After: a supplement* (1979), vol. XXIX: 122–123, London: Macmillan for the Royal Economic Society.

—— (1934b) 'A note on the dynamic pricing problem', stencil dated Gothenburg 23 October 1934; reprinted in *The Collected Writings of J.M. Keynes, the* General Theory *and After: a supplement* (1979), vol. XXIX: 123–131, London: Macmillan for the Royal Economic Society.

—— (1939) 'The dynamic approach to economic theory', in *Studies in the Theory of Money and Capital*, London: George Allen and Unwin.

Mahloudji, F. (1985) 'Hicks and the Keynesian revolution', *History of Political Economy*, 17(2): 287–307.

Marshall, A. (1890, 8th edn 1920) *Principles of Economics*, London: Macmillan.

Mata, T.J.F. (2004) 'Constructing identity: the Post Keynesians and the capital controversies', *Journal of the History of Economic Thought*, 26(2): 241–259.

Meade, J. (1936–1937) 'A simplified model of Mr. Keynes's system,' *Review of Economic Studies*, 4(1): 98–107.

Messori, M. (1991) 'Keynes' *General Theory* and the endogenous money supply', *Économie Appliquée*, 44(1): 125–152.

Milgate, M. (1982) *Capital and Employment: a study of Keynes's economics*, London: Academic Press.

Minsky, H.P. (1975) *John Maynard Keynes*, New York: Columbia University Press.

—— (1977) 'The financial instability hypothesis: an interpretation of Keynes and an alternative to "standard theory"', *Challenge*, 20(1): 20–35.

Moore, B.J. (1983) 'Unpacking the Post Keynesian black box: bank lending and the money supply', *Journal of Post Keynesian Economics*, 5(4): 537–556; reprinted in M.C. Sawyer (ed.) (1988) *Post-Keynesian Economics*, Aldershot: Edward Elgar; also in M. Musella and C. Panico (eds) (1995) *The Money Supply in the Economic Process: a Post Keynesian perspective*, Aldershot: Edward Elgar.

—— (1988) *Horizontalists and Verticalists: the macroeconomics of credit money*, Cambridge: Cambridge University Press.

—— (1991) 'Money supply endogeneity: "reserve price setting" or "reserve quantity setting"?', *Journal of Post Keynesian Economics*, 13(3): 404–413.

—— (1995) 'The exogeneity of short-term interest rates: a reply to Wray', *Journal of Economic Issues*, 29(1): 258–266.

Musella, M. and Panico, C. (eds) (1995) *The Money Supply in the Economic Process: a Post Keynesian perspective*, Aldershot: Edward Elgar.

Nasica, E. and Kregel, J.A. (1999) 'Alternative analyses of uncertainty and rationality: Keynes and modern economics', in S. Marzetti Dall'Aste Brandolin and R. Scazzieri (eds) *La Probabilità in Keynes: premesse ed influenze*, Bologna: Clueb.

Niggle, C.J. (1991) 'The endogenous money supply theory: an institutionalist appraisal', *Journal of Economic Issues*, 25(1): 137–51; reprinted in M. Musella and C. Panico (eds) (1995) *The Money Supply in the Economic Process: a Post Keynesian perspective*, Aldershot: Edward Elgar.

O'Donnell, R.M. (1989) *Keynes: philosophy, economics and politics*, London: Macmillan.

—— (1997) 'Keynes and formalism,' in G.C. Harcourt and P.A. Riach (eds) *A 'Second Edition' of the General Theory*, vol. 2, London: Routledge.

Palley, T.I. (1991) 'The endogenous money supply: consensus and disagreement', *Journal of Post Keynesian Economics*, 13(3): 397–403.

—— (1994) 'Competing views of the money supply: theory and evidence', *Metroeconomica*, 45(1): 67–88.

—— (1996a) 'Accommodationism versus structuralism: time for an accommodation', *Journal of Post Keynesian Economics*, 18(4): 585–594.

—— (1996b) 'The emergence of theoretical and institutional coherence in Post

Keynesian economics', in *Post Keynesian Economics: debt, distribution and the macro economy* (1996), London: Macmillan Press.

—— (1996c) *Post Keynesian Economics: debt, distribution and the macro economy*, London: Macmillan Press.

Panico, C. and Petri, F. (1987) 'Long-run and short-run', in J. Eatwell, M. Milgate and P. Newman (eds) *The New Palgrave: a dictionary of economics*, London: Palgrave Macmillan.

Parguez, A. (1984) 'La dynamique de la monnaie', *Économies et Sociétés, Monnaie et Production*, 1(4): 83–118.

—— (1996) 'Beyond scarcity: a reappraisal of the theory of the monetary circuit', in G. Deleplace and E.J. Nell (eds) *Money in Motion: the Post Keynesian and Circulation Approaches*, London: Macmillan Press.

Parguez, A. and Seccareccia, M. (2000) 'The Credit Theory of Money: the monetary circuit approach', in J. Smithin (ed.) *What is Money?*, London: Routledge.

Pasinetti, L. (1974) *Growth and Income Distribution: essays in economic theory*, Cambridge: Cambridge University Press.

—— (1999) 'J.M. Keynes's "revolution": the major event of the twentieth-century economics?', in L. Pasinetti and B. Schefold (eds) *The Impact of Keynes on Economics in the 20th Century*, Cheltenham: Edward Elgar.

—— (2005) 'The Cambridge school of Keynesian economics', *Cambridge Journal of Economics*, 29(6): 837–848.

—— (2007) *Keynes and the Cambridge Keynesians: a 'revolution in economics' to be accomplished*, Cambridge: Cambridge University Press.

Pekkarinen, J. (1986) 'Early Hicks and Keynesian monetary theory: different views on liquidity preference', *History of Political Economy*, 18(2): 335–349.

Pollin, R. (1991) 'Two theories of money supply endogeneity: some empirical evidence', *Journal of Post Keynesian Economics*, 13(3): 366–396.

—— (1996) 'Money supply endogeneity: what are the questions and why do they matter?', in G. Deleplace and E.J. Nell (eds) *Money in Motion: the Post Keynesian and Circulation approaches*, London: Macmillan.

Post Keynesianism (2005) *Journal of Post Keynesian Economics*, Special Issue, Spring, 27(3).

Pratten, S. (2005) 'Economics as progress: the LSE approach to econometric modelling and critical realism as programmes for research', *Cambridge Journal of Economics*, 29(2): 179–205.

Rabin, M. and Thaler, R.H. (2001) 'Anomalies: risk aversion', *Journal of Economic Perspectives*, 15(1): 219–232.

Realfonzo R. (1998) *Money and Banking: theory and debate (1900–1940)*, Cheltenham: Edward Elgar.

Robinson, J. (1937) *Essays in the Theory of Employment*, London: Macmillan.

—— (1942) *An Essay on Marxian Economics*, London: Macmillan.

—— (1949) 'Mr. Harrod's dynamics', *Economic Journal*, 59(233): 68–85; reprinted in *Collected Economic Papers* (1951), vol. 1, Oxford: Basil Blackwell.

—— (1953–54) 'The production function and the theory of capital', *Review of Economic Studies*, 21(2): 81–106; reprinted in *Collected Economic Papers* (1960), vol. 2, Oxford: Basil Blackwell.

—— (1956) *The Accumulation of Capital*, London: Macmillan.

—— (1962) *Essays in the Theory of Economic Growth*, London: Macmillan.

—— (1970) 'Quantity theories old and new: a comment', *Journal of Money, Credit and Banking*, 2(4): 504–512.

—— (1971) *Economic Heresies: some old-fashioned questions in economic theory*, London: Macmillan.

—— (1972) 'The second crisis of economic theory', *American Economic Review*, Papers and Proceedings, 62(2): 1–10; reprinted in *Collected Economic Papers* (1973), vol. 4, Oxford: Basil Blackwell.

—— (1974) 'History versus equilibrium', *Thames Papers in Political Economy*, London: Thames Polytechnic; reprinted in *Collected Economic Papers* (1979), vol. 5, Oxford: Basil Blackwell.

—— (1978) 'Keynes and Ricardo', *Journal of Post Keynesian Economics*, 1(1): 12–18; reprinted in *Collected Economic Papers* (1979), vol. 5: 110–119, Oxford: Basil Blackwell.

—— (1979) 'Thinking about thinking', in *Collected Economic Papers* (1979), vol. 5, Oxford: Basil Blackwell.

Robinson, J. and Eatwell, J. (1973) *Introduction to Modern Economics*, Maidenhead: McGraw-Hill.

Rochon, L.P. (1999a) 'The creation and circulation of endogenous money: a circuit dynamic approach', *Journal of Economic Issues*, 33(1): 1–21.

—— (1999b) *Credit, Money and Production: an alternative Post-Keynesian approach*, Cheltenham: Edward Elgar.

—— (2000) '1939–1958: was Kaldor an endogenist?', *Metroeconomica*, 51(2): 191–220.

Rochon L.P. and Rossi S. (eds) (2003) *Modern Theories of Money: the nature and role of money in capitalist economies*, Cheltenham: Edward Elgar.

Rochon, L.P. and Vernengo, M. (eds) (2001) *Credit, Interest Rates and the Open Economy*, Cheltenham: Edward Elgar.

Roncaglia, A. (1978) *Sraffa and the Theory of Prices*, Chichester: Wiley.

Rossi, S. (1998) 'Endogenous money and banking activity: some notes on the workings of modern payment systems', *Studi Economici*, 53(3): 23–56.

—— (2001) *Money and Inflation: a new macroeconomic analysis*, Cheltenham: Edward Elgar.

Rotheim, R.J. (1988) 'Keynes and the language of probability and uncertainty', *Journal of Post Keynesian Economics*, 11(1): 82–99.

—— (ed.) (1998) *New Keynesian Economics – Post Keynesian Alternatives*, London: Routledge.

Rottenstreich, Y. and Tversky, A. (1997) 'Unpacking, repacking, and anchoring: advances in support theory', *Psychology Review*, 104(2): 406–415.

Runde, J. (1990) 'Keynesian uncertainty and the weight of arguments', *Economics and Philosophy*, 6(2): 275–292.

—— (1991) 'Keynesian uncertainty and the instability of beliefs', *Review of Political Economy*, 3(2): 125–145.

Samuels, W. J. (1993) 'John R. Hicks and the history of economics', *History of Political Economy*, 25(2): 351–374.

Samuelson, P.A. (1968) 'What Classical and Neoclassical monetary theory really was', *Canadian Journal of Economics*, 1(1): 1–15.

Sardoni, C. (1989) 'Chapter 18 of the *General Theory*: its methodological importance', *Journal of Post Keynesian Economics*, 12(2): 293–307.

Sawyer, M.C. (1985) *The Economics of Michal Kalecki*, London: Macmillan.

—— (ed.) (1988) *Post-Keynesian Economics*, Aldershot: Edward Elgar.

—— (1991) 'Post-Keynesian economics: the state of the art', in W. Adriaansen and J. Van der Linden (eds) (1991) *Post-Keynesian Thought in Perspective*, Amsterdam: Wolters-Noordhoff.

—— (1996) 'Money, finance and interest rates', in P. Arestis (ed.) *Keynes, Money and the Open Economy: essays in honour of Paul Davidson*, Cheltenham: Edward Elgar.

—— (2001a) 'Kalecki on money and finance', *European Journal of the History of Economic Thought*, 8(4): 487–508.

—— (2001b) 'Kalecki on imperfect competition, inflation and money', *Cambridge Journal of Economics*, 25(2): 245–261.

Schumpeter, J.A. (1912) *Theorie der wirtschaftlichen Entwicklung*, Leipzig: Duncker & Humblot; trans. *The Theory of Economic Development* (1934), Cambridge, MA: Harvard University Press.

Seidman, L. (2003) *Automatic Fiscal Policies to Combact Recessions*, London: M.E. Sharpe.

Shackle, G.L.S. (1961) *Decision, Order and Time in Human Affairs*, Cambridge: Cambridge University Press.

—— (1967) *The Years of High Theory*, Cambridge: Cambridge University Press.

—— (1971) 'Foundations of monetary policy: discussion paper', in G. Clayton, J.C. Gilbert and R. Sedwick (eds) *Monetary Theory and Monetary Policy in the 1970s*, Oxford: Oxford University Press.

—— (1991) 'Book review of *A Market Theory of Money* by John Hicks', *Review of Political Economy*, 3(3): 354.

Smithin, J. (1994) *Controversies in Monetary Economics: ideas, issues and policy*, Aldershot: Edward Elgar.

Smithin, J. (ed.) (2000) *What is Money?*, London: Routledge.

Solow, R.M. (1984) 'Mr. Hicks and the Classics', in D.A. Collard *et al.* (eds) *Economic Theory and Hicksian Themes*, Oxford: Oxford University Press.

Sraffa, P. (1960) *The Production of Commodities by Means of Commodities*, Cambridge: Cambridge University Press.

Starmer, C. (1999) 'Experimental economics: hard science or wasteful tinkering?' *Economic Journal*, 109(453): F5–F15.

Stiglitz, J. (2002) 'Information and the change in the paradigm in economics', *American Economic Review*, 92(3): 460–501.

Targetti, F. and Kinda-Hass, B. (1982) 'Kalecki's review of Keynes's *General Theory*', *Australian Economic Papers*, 21(39): 245–260.

Thirlwall, A.P. (1987) *Nicholas Kaldor*, Brighton: Harvester.

Tily, G. (2007) *Keynes's General Theory, the Rate of Interest and 'Keynesian' Economics*, Basingstoke: Palgrave Macmillan.

Tversky, A. and Kahneman, D. (1974) 'Judgment under uncertainty: heuristics and biases', *Science*, 185(4157): 1124–1131.

—— (1983) 'Extensional versus intuitive reasoning: the conjunction fallacy in probability judgement', *Psychological Review*, 90(4): 293–315.

Wallich, H.C. and Weintraub, S. (1971) 'A tax-based incomes policy', *Journal of Economic Issues*, 5(2): 1–19.

Walters, B. and Young, D. (1997) 'On the coherence of Post-Keynesian economics', *Scottish Journal of Political Economy*, 44(3): 329–349.

Weintraub, S. (1958) *An Approach to the Theory of Income Distribution*, Philadelphia: Chilton.

—— (1959) *A General Theory of the Price Level, Output, Income Distribution and Economic Growth*, Philadelphia: Chilton.

—— (ed.) (1978) *Keynes, Keynesians, and Monetarists*, Philadelphia: University of Pennsylvania Press.

Wicksell, K. (1898) *Geldzins und Güterpreise. Eine Studie über die den Tauschwert des Geldes bestimmenden Ursachen*, Jena: G. Fischer; trans. by R.F. Kahn as *Interest and Prices: A Study of the Causes Regulating the Value of Money* (1936), London: Macmillan.

Winslow, E.G. (1986) 'Human logic and Keynes's economics', *Eastern Economic Journal*, 12(4): 413–430.

Wolfson, M. (1996) 'A Post Keynesian theory of credit rationing', *Journal of Post Keynesian Economics*, 18(3): 443–470.

Wood, A. (1975) *A Theory of Profits*, Cambridge: Cambridge University Press.

Woodford, M. (2002) 'Financial markets efficiency and the effectiveness of monetary policy', *FRBNY Economic Policy Review*, 8(1): 85–94.

Wray, L.R. (1990) *Money and Credit in Capitalist Economies: the endogenous money approach*, Aldershot: Edward Elgar.

—— (1992) 'Commercial banks, the central bank, and endogenous money', *Journal of Post Keynesian Economics*, 14(3): 297–310.

—— (1995) 'Keynesian monetary theory: liquidity preference or black box horizontalism?', *Journal of Economic Issues*, 29(1): 273–283.

—— (1998) *Understanding Modern Money: the key to full employment and price stability*, Cheltenham: Edward Elgar.

Young, W. (1987) *Interpreting Mr. Keynes: the IS-LM enigma*, Oxford: Basil Blackwell.

Index

For Product Safety Concerns and Information please contact our EU representative GPSR@taylorandfrancis.com Taylor & Francis Verlag GmbH, Kaufingerstraße 24, 80331 München, Germany

T - #0124 - 160425 - C0 - 216/138/9 - PB - 9780415588737 - Gloss Lamination